49 CITIES

KEY TO DIAGRAMS

Fear Factor

FOREIGN INVASION

DISORGANIZED TRAFFIC

SLUMS + OVERCROWDING

SPRAWL

URBAN CHAOS

INFLEXIBILITY

POLLUTED AIR

WASTE OF RESOURCES

Form

LINEAR

GRID

RADIAL

IRREGULAR

Realization

UNBUILT

PARTIALLY BUILT, OR INFLUENTIAL ON OTHER BUILT PROJECTS

COMPLETELY BUILT

Expandability

WALLED CITY

MODERATE GROWTH

UNLIMITED GROWTH

WILDERNESS

PUBLIC GREENSPACE (PARK)

PRIVATE GREENSPACE (LAWN)

AGRICULTURE

WATER

INDUSTRY

HOUSING

PUBLIC/ COMMERCIAL

PEDESTRIAN DECK

ROADS/ INFRASTRUCTURE

OTHER INFRASTRUCTURE

49 CITIES

WORKac

Third Edition

With contributions from
Yona Friedman
Sam Jacob
Chip Lord
Curtis Schreier
Michael Webb

INVENTORY PRESS

Mound, 1964

Fun Palace, 1965

Frankfurt, 1963

Ratingen-West, 1965

Clusters in the Air, 1962

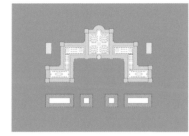

Royal Salt Works, 1775

Phalanstère, 1800

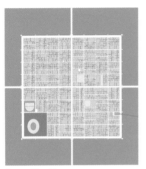

Roman City, -50

Marienburg, 1890

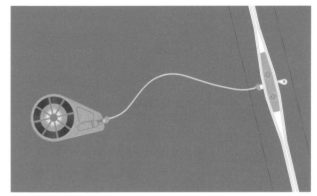

Convention City, 1972

Satellite City, 1965

Fort Worth, 1956

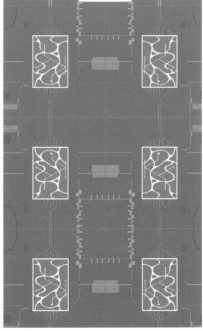

No-Stop City, 1969

SCALE COMPARISONS 1:25,000

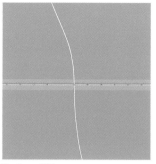

Roadtown, 1910

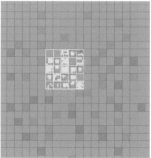

Agricultural City, 1960

Bridge-Town Over the Channel, 1963

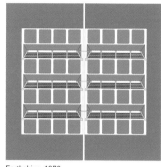

Earthships, 1970

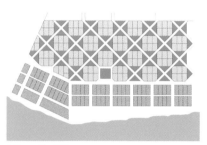

Jeffersonville, 1802

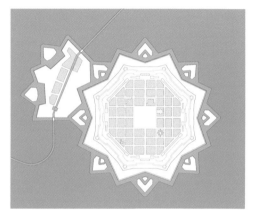

Neuf-Brisach, 1700

Zarzis Resort, 1974

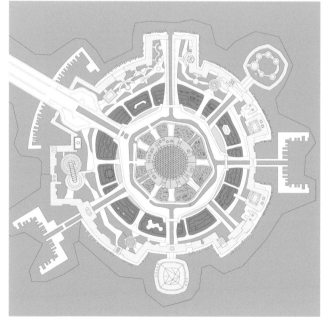

Noahbabel, 1969

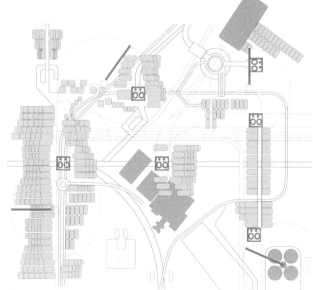

Plug-in City, 1964

1 = 25,000

7

Latin American City, 1650

Levittown, 1958

Le Mirail, 1962

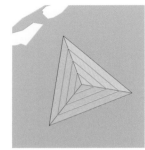

Exodus, 1972

Tetrahedral City, 1965

Masdar City, 2006–

Hauptstadt, 1958

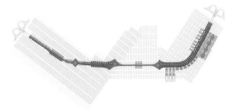

Linear City, 1967

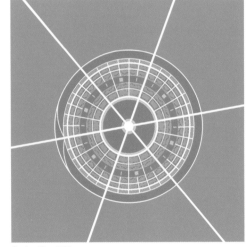

Garden City, 1902

New Babylon, 1960

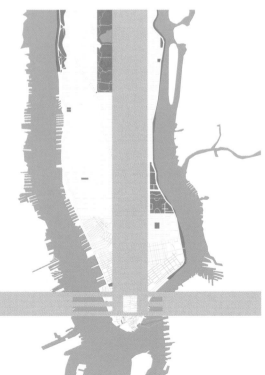

Continuous Monument, 1969

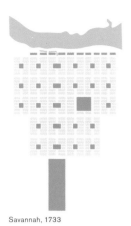

Savannah, 1733

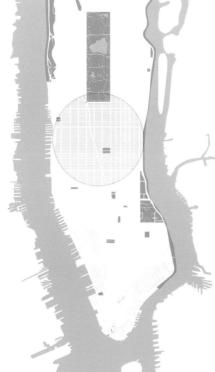

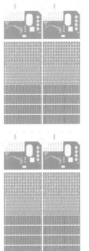

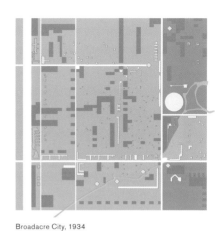

Broadacre City, 1934

Rush City Reformed, 1923

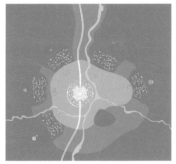

Handloser, 1973

Dome over Manhattan, 1960

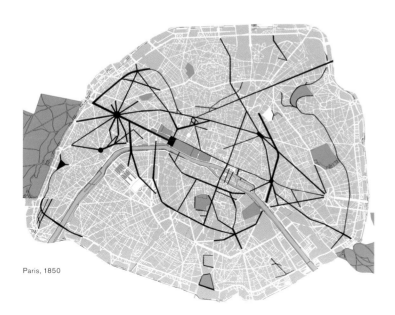

Paris, 1850

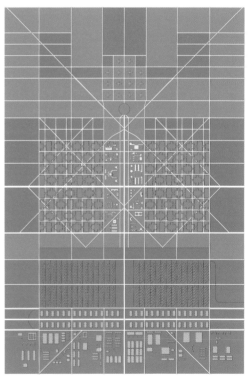

Radiant City, 1935

1 = 133,000

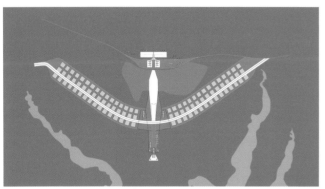

Brasilia, 1957

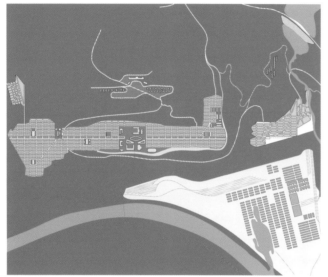

Cité Industrielle, 1917

Ocean City, 1960

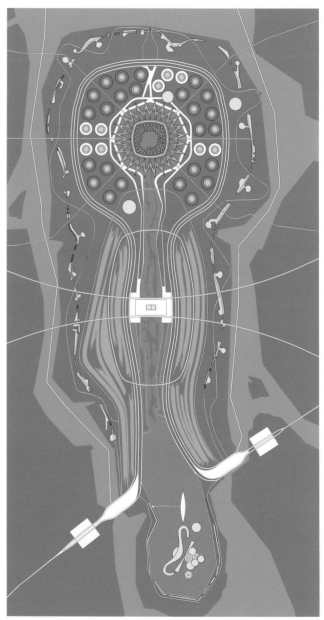

Mesa City, 1960

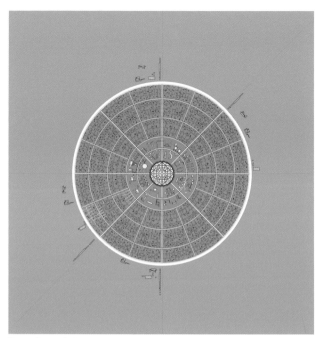

Communitas 1, 1947

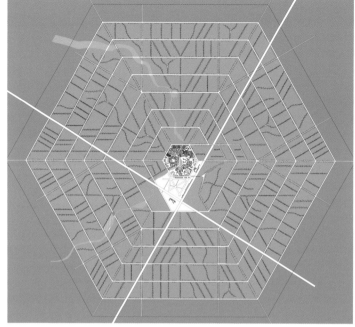

Communitas 2, 1947

Tokyo Bay, 1960

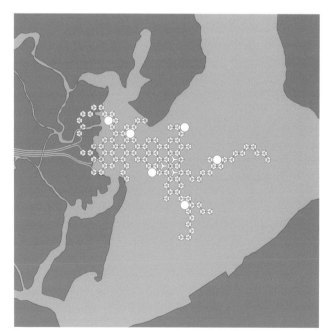

Helix City, 1961

1 = 250,000

FEAR TIMELINE

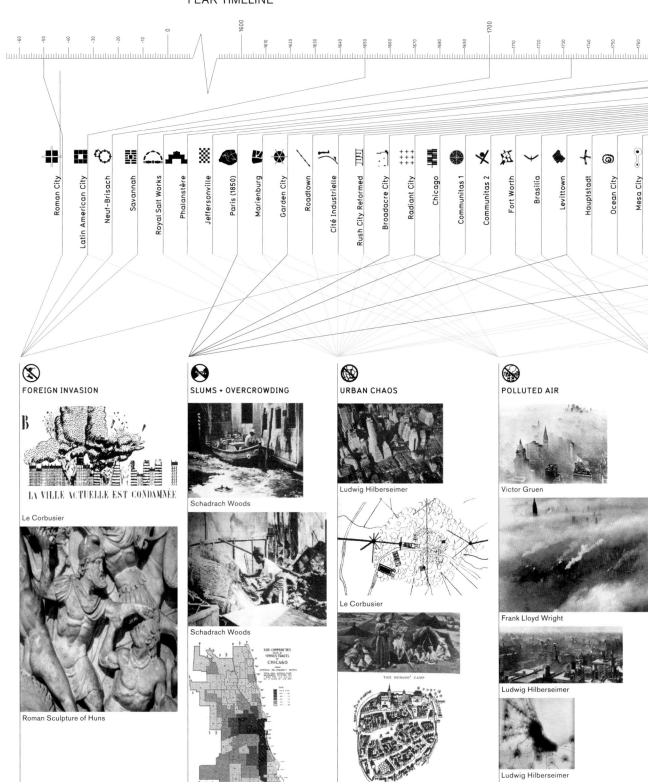

Roman City · Latin American City · Neuf-Brisach · Savannah · Royal Salt Works · Phalanstère · Jeffersonville · Paris (1850) · Marienburg · Garden City · Roadtown · Cité Industrielle · Rush City Reformed · Broadacre City · Radiant City · Chicago · Communitas 1 · Communitas 2 · Fort Worth · Brasilia · Levittown · Hauptstadt · Ocean City · Mesa City

FOREIGN INVASION

LA VILLE ACTUELLE EST CONDAMNÉE
Le Corbusier

Roman Sculpture of Huns

SLUMS + OVERCROWDING

Schadrach Woods

Schadrach Woods

Ludwig Hilberseimer

URBAN CHAOS

Ludwig Hilberseimer

Le Corbusier

Le Corbusier

POLLUTED AIR

Victor Gruen

Frank Lloyd Wright

Ludwig Hilberseimer

Ludwig Hilberseimer

FEAR TIMELINE

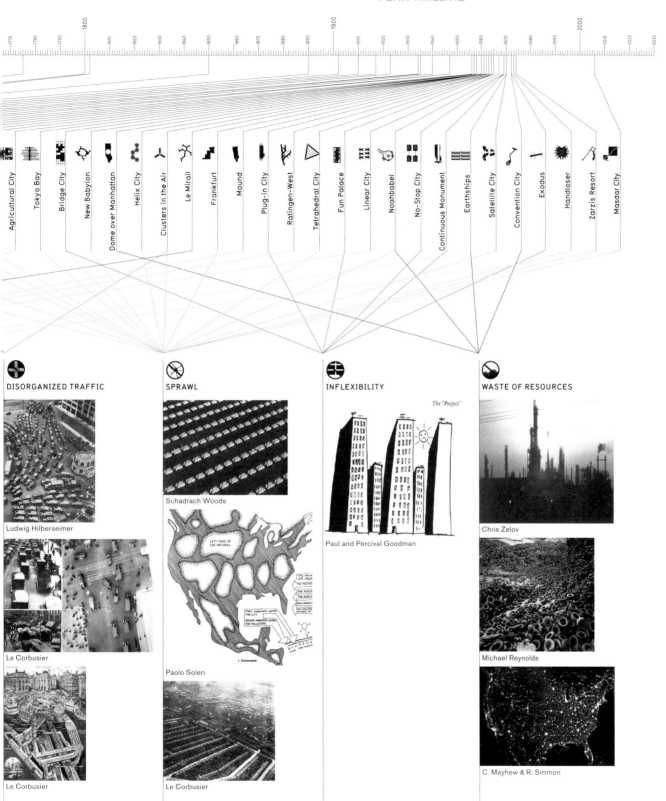

DISORGANIZED TRAFFIC

Ludwig Hilberseimer

Le Corbusier

Le Corbusier

SPRAWL

Schadrach Woods

Paolo Soleri

Le Corbusier

INFLEXIBILITY

The "Project"

Paul and Percival Goodman

WASTE OF RESOURCES

Chris Zelov

Michael Reynolds

C. Mayhew & R. Simmon

PREFACE TO THE THIRD EDITION

Amale Andraos
Dan Wood

The research that eventually became *49 Cities* was done during the summer of 2007. Initially, we saw this work a way for us to look at the history of urbanism differently, through what we called at the time an "ecological lens." However, we did not know exactly what this meant, or what we were looking for.

Through the relatively simple process of research, data collection, and—most importantly—redrawing the plans to scale within a coded color palette, we eventually came to understand these projects with a degree of complexity that perhaps even their authors had not. Being able to compare the different cities in such an immediate way allowed us to discover new patterns and themes.

We came to understand, for example, the importance of infrastructure—from streets to sewers to photovoltaic fields—in the development of urban form. By using only original sources, we rediscovered details such as the vegetable gardens in La Ville Radieuse that had been lost to history. And by including many pre-industrial projects, we saw the changes and developments in thinking about the relationship between a city and its more rural surroundings, a crucial factor before the advent of refrigeration and industrial-scaled agriculture.

These observations have had an enormous impact on our own thinking and design process. The very first sketches of our project Public Farm 1 for MoMA/PS1, which we built in 2008, were inspired by the projects in *49 Cities*—a vision of urban agriculture as a new form of infrastructure, a "farm-bridge" floating above the city. Public Farm 1 was the first project that allowed us to clearly announce—and build—our own agenda, independent of program or market demands. Other projects followed, including the theoretical Locavore Fantasia and Plug-Out, master plans that transformed sustainable infrastructure into organizing principals for new cities, other research projects such as New Ark or Infoodstructure that looked at food production and cities, and our current work creating gardens and kitchen classroom buildings in each of New York's five boroughs for Edible Schoolyard NYC.

Since completing the research, however, we had always wanted to try our hand at designing a "50th City." In 2012, we were finally afforded that opportunity with the invitation to participate in MoMA's exhibition *Foreclosed: Rehousing the American Dream*. Our project, Nature-City, reinvents Ebenezer Howards Town Country for the twenty-first century, reimagining the suburbs of Keizer, Oregon. We enlisted a team that included civil engineers, economic analysts, the conservation ecologist Eric Sanderson, and the law professor Gerald Frug, an expert on local government law and public space.

True to the data-centric approach of *49 Cities*, we were able to create a new enclave for 14,000 residents that is more than five times as dense as the suburbs that surround it, while at the same time providing three times as much open green space. A multiplicity of housing options were designed, with each major structure doubling as infrastructure and using the particularities of its infrastructural function to create new typologies (a hill-dwelling, for example, that surrounds a methane dome collecting gas from the city's composted waste and using excess heat for a series of neighborhood pools on the roof).

The lessons and discoveries tracing their origins to *49 Cities* continue in our office to this day. Another building imagined for Nature-City, for example, created water pressure for the city through giant interior waterfalls, an idea we have reused in designing a waterfall for the grey water system in our project for a new conference center in Gabon.

Featuring a new interview and insights from culture-defining architect Yona Friedman, as well as an in-depth conversation with Chip Lord and Curtis Schreier of Ant Farm, we hope that with this third edition, a new generation of architects, urban designers, and students will be able to mine its data to imagine and create their own worlds and hopefully discover ways to make our future cities more habitable, responsible, and visionary.

Public Farm 1, WORKac, 2008.

Top: Nature City Caverns/Tower of Houses, WORKac, 2012.
Bottom: Nature City Compost Hill, WORKac, 2012.

INTRODUCTION

Amale Andraos

Throughout history, architects and planners have dreamed of "better" and different cities—more flexible, more controllable, more defensible, more efficient, more monumental, more organic, taller, denser, sparser, or greener. With every plan, radical visions were proposed, ones that embodied not only the desires but also, and more often, the fears and anxieties of their time.

With the failure of the suburban experiment and the looming end-of-the-world predictions—from global warming to post peak-oil energy crises and uncontrolled world urbanization—architects and urbanists find themselves once more at a crossroads, fertile for visionary thinking. Today's meeting of intensified environmental fears with the global breakdown of laissez-faire capitalism has produced a new kind of audience, one that is ready to suspend disbelief and engage in fantastic projections to radically rethink the way we live.

Recognizing the recurrent nature of our environmental preoccupations and their impact in shaping utopias, 49 Cities inscribes our time within a larger historical context, rereading seminal projects and visionary cities of the past through an ecological lens of the present that goes beyond their declared ideology to compare and contrast their hypothetical ecological footprint. And while both terms constituting the research—that of "city" and that of "ecology"—are purposefully reduced almost to naïveté, they are still powerful enough in their simplicity to reveal that many of these radical propositions are closer than we are today in boldly articulating the challenges we face and offering inspiring possibilities to meet them.

Born out of our "eco-urbanism" research seminar at Princeton University's School of Architecture, 49 Cities emerged as a means to re-engage thinking about the city and reclaim architects' imagination towards reinventing both urban and rural life. While initially focused on the present condition, analyzing current trends in green architecture and urbanism, our interest gradually gravitated back in time, towards the long tradition of prolific visionary thinking about the city that was lost sometime in the mid-1970s. Encouraged by the "amateur-planner" status of those who dreamed of the most influential plans—

from Frank Lloyd Wright and Le Corbusier, who were architects, to Ebeneezer Howard, who was a stenographer—and unconvinced by more recent professional manifestos such as that of the New Urbanists, we set ourselves to find ways to move beyond mapping our "urban-on-speed" condition and rediscover alternate modes to re-project the city.

The forty-nine cities were selected amongst two hundred cases studied, based on their ability to capture a time and an ambition, by either best representing their contemporaries or by being radically ahead of their time. Some cities were built in one form or another, but most of them remained on paper. And yet today, many have indelibly influenced our global urban landscape. While the repercussions of Radiant City, Broadacre City, and Garden City have been widely acknowledged, it is interesting to compare recent developments in China and the UAE to some of these visionary plans, ranging from the more utilitarian to the more exuberant. These parallels stop at form: while today's urban developments are almost always shaped by capital flows, the forty-nine cities were all shaped by ideology and an ambition to recast society's modes of being and operation, an ambition that produced widely varying results depending on their time and place.

Beyond their particularities and specific preoccupations, there are two characteristics that most of the forty-nine cities share. The first lies in the embrace of scale and radical abstraction to question their impact on the planet as a whole. A better city for the future always seems to imply a redefined relationship to "nature" and the environment, a relationship whose form—whether it requires sprawl to embrace wilderness or compression to minimize impact—depends on the broader ideology it embodies. The second is that each of the forty-nine cities is born as a reaction to the urban conditions and preoccupations of the time—overpopulation, sprawl, chaos, slums, pollution, or war.

With today's heightened fear of upcoming environmental disasters, "ecological urbanism" seems the natural first utopia of the twenty-first century. Projecting today's questions about what constitutes an ideal "ecological city" on

to the idealized cities of the past, 49 Cities examines a number of relationships—from the relationship of form to ideology to that of form to performance—generating a fresh outlook and a new framework from which to re-engage the discourse on the city today.

FINDINGS

Dan Wood

49 Cities is organized chronologically, categorized in terms of the cities' overall form (linear, gridded, radial, or irregular) and "fear factor"–the predominant conditions that each city is imagined to overcome or alleviate (foreign invasions, sprawl, urban chaos, slums, inflexibility, pollution, or waste). Each city has been carefully redrawn. There is a key to the diagrams on the inside front cover of the book.

Using these drawings and available information, each city is subjected to a quantitative analysis, calculating the overall area, population, amount of greenspace, water and infrastructure as well as floor area ratio and both two-dimensional (footprint) and three-dimensional (surface area) densities. The cities are then ranked in a number of categories–from 1 to 49–in order to compare and contrast the different approaches.

FORM

The ultimate expression of urbanity, the grid, appears again and again, recognizable as the dominant urban form in twenty of the forty-nine cities, and used as the basis of designs meant to combat everything from pollution to inflexibility. The grid transcends time and geography, serving projects as diverse as Wright's Broadacre City and Le Corbusier's Radiant City. In an unintended symmetry in fact, the newest of the forty-nine cities, Foster's Masdar, takes many of its urban design cues from the oldest, the Roman city.

The grid is the only form used when the fear factor is foreign invasion or warfare, its aura of control and organization dating back to the Roman Empire. The diversity of uses and expressions of gridded cities however, from the Conquistadors in Latin America to Archizoom, is testament to the grid's ultimate flexibility, suiting the needs of both colonialists and radicals.

Eleven of the forty-nine cities take on irregular forms, from Kitutake's Ocean City, inspired by organic structures, to Haussman's interventions in Paris, which follow the city's informal historic development. Given the identification of irregular forms with informality and open-endedness, it is ironic that almost all of the authors of these cities conceived of them as antidotes to perceived urban chaos or

sprawl. Many of the more geometric or tightly organized cities have a greater density or potential to expand, however, showing perhaps the danger of becoming seduced by the organic when searching for a more balanced state of urban coexistence with nature.

Another eleven cities are organized linearly. The earliest example is 1910's Roadtown and in many ways it is still the most revolutionary, designed as a continuous collection of row-houses, rail lines, and a roadway stretching from Baltimore to Washington. Later examples, such as the Metabolists' projects use the linear form within an organic argument, organizing the city by "trunk," "branch," "stem," and "leaves." Linear cities are inherently inflexible, expandable only in one dimension and singular in expression, yet all of them share a fascination with infrastructure, making them potential models for future ecological cities whose infrastructural systems will require reinvention.

The radial form is the least used, appearing in seven of the cities studied. However, from Ledoux's Saltworks to the Communitas projects of Paul and Percival Goodman, it provides perhaps the most compelling "visionary" form, one that combines the structure and flexibility of a grid with the curved organic forms of nature. The limit to endless radial expansion can in some sense be a benefit, allowing for new settlements to be separated by open space, agriculture, or wilderness such as was originally proposed by Howard for his Garden Cities.

DENSITY

No urban quality reflects the ecological promise of visionary cities better than density. As more and more people crowd the planet–and move to cities–it is imperative to find innovative ways to occupy less space with more people. Urban visionaries from Doxiadis to MVRDV, and many of the authors of the forty-nine cities have trumpeted denser cities as the solution to any number of societal and ecological ills.

The densities of the forty-nine cities have been calculated using either their stated population goals or by estimating the number of residential units. For the four projects that encompass an existing commercial area however (Candillis Wood's Frankfurt, the Smithsons'

Hauptstadt, Buckminster Fuller's Dome over Manhattan, and Victor Gruen's Fort Worth), the number of users/commuters is estimated instead, which skews these numbers higher than the population density calculated for the others.

Topping the list of the densest, and true to form, is Fuller's Tetrahedral City of 1965. Fuller postulated that a pyramidal structure 200-stories tall with a giant public park inside would not only be able to house one million people in 300,000 apartments, but that the structure would also be light enough to float. (He proposed this for both Tokyo and San Francisco bays.) Cedric Price's Fun Palace is the next densest, followed by Archigram's Plug-in City. Both of these projects herald the High Tech movement by incorporating small, efficient modules that are able to accommodate great numbers of people on a reduced footprint. Rounding out the top five are Superstudio's Continuous Monument and Archizoom's No-Stop City, both highly theoretical projects meant to transform the lives of vast numbers of people on one level–Superstudio stated that the Continuous Monument should house the global population–and on another level, meant more as social critique than urban planning.

No one in the 1960s and 1970s championed the environmental city and the merits of density more than Paolo Soleri. He introduced his book *Arcology: City in the Image of Man* (1969) with the statement "miniaturize or die." Analyzing the two Soleri projects included in *49 Cities*, Noahbabel and Mesa City, it is therefore surprising that neither project is particularly dense. Mesa City, in fact, is one of the least dense in terms of surface area.

FAR

Floor area ratio, or FAR, represents the number of times the entire urban footprint is duplicated in total built area. Cities with a high FAR also have a high 3-D density. For the projects that are megastructures–such as Peter Cook's Mound or Cedric Price's Fun Palace–the FAR is simply equal to the number of floors; these projects have the highest FARs. (Tetrahedral City, again, tops the list–it is hard to beat a 200-story pyramid.) Existing cities like Fort

Worth, or Dome over Manhattan, also score highly in FAR calculations, as both of these projects cover commercial centers with little or no open space.

Soleri's projects make up in FAR what they lack in density, but this is because Soleri's Arcologies are often limited to the structures themselves, with little attention to their surrounding areas, assumed to be wilderness. High density/high FAR approaches can conceivably be combined with larger and more generous open space, while still accommodating large populations, a possible approach to the cities of the future.

POPULATION

Total population is the stated or calculated number of people for which the city has been designed. It shows the breadth of ambition of the project, and can also be read as analogous to the ego of the visionary. Some projects are absolutely mammoth in terms of numbers. Kenzo Tange's Tokyo Bay project is designed for five million people, expandable to accommodate ten million. The Goodmans' Communitas projects are envisioned as cities of six million people engaged in "efficient consumption." Hilberseimer's pre-suburban dispersal plan for Chicago calls for moving four million people out of the city center in order to minimize the effects of a nuclear bomb dropped in the downtown core. Soleri and Le Corbusier both tackle cities of approximately two million. A few projects—such as Isozaki's Clusters in the Air of 1962 or Roadtown—turn out to have much smaller capacities than one would have imagined.

OPEN SPACE

In all forty-nine cities, open space is clearly an equal focus to built space—whether the two are intertwined or one is compressed to allow for the other's expansion. Cities that overtly deal with rural areas, such as Kurokawa's Agricultural City or Handloser by Richard Snibbe, score highly, as do Howard's Garden City and the Communitas projects, which both imagine a balance between surrounding open land and developed cities. Le Corbusier's Radiant City calls for every building to have both public space at the rooftops and pilotis at the base,

allowing the ground to continue beneath the buildings, which creates a city with 100 percent of the footprint dedicated as open space or greenspace, equaled only by Peter Cook's Mound—a city completely buried in a hill.

AVERAGES

While ecological cities cannot be measured by data alone and density, population, FAR, and percentage greenspace may not be the only, or the most important measurers of sustainability, it is obvious that a green city of the future must address all of these issues head-on.

It is useful, therefore, to look at those cities that achieved consistency in all categories by averaging their rankings. Unexpectedly, Le Corbusier's Radiant City scores the highest, followed closely by Fuller's Tetrahedral City. The two visionaries are in many ways at the opposite ends of the rationalist spectra: Fuller, the scientist and inventor convinced that geometry and efficiency provided the keys for a future society based on equality and temp- erance, and Le Corbusier, the artist and architect whose intuitive drive to discover the essence of the new modern world drove him to imagine a city of sunlight and open spaces, while at the same time providing the foundation for the inert and oppressive regime of faceless urban redevelopment of the 1970s. While Fuller is often hailed as a genius whose time perhaps is yet to come, Le Corbusier remains vilified in many quarters for his urban visions: a quote from *Ville Radieuse* provides the introduction to the New Urbanist tract *Suburban Nation*, which goes on to lay all of America's urban problems at the French master's feet.

So while it is perhaps no surprise that Fuller's musings led to one of the densest, most efficient (and strangest) visions of urbanity in *49 Cities*, Radiant City's performance seems to open an opportunity to rediscover and perhaps reread the project through our ecological lens. Consistently referring to his project as "La Ville Verte"—the Green City—Le Corbusier discusses his plan as a means to combat pollution, provide light and open greenspace as well as house vast numbers of people humanely. Putting aside his insistence on the separation of uses, one can almost imagine

the Radiant City being argued as a means to combat climate change and deal with our current pace of urbanization.

There are also unexpected twists in some of the most familiar elements of the Ville Radieuse, beginning with the notion of "Towers in the Park." Le Corbusier's greenspaces are much different from the pale grass plazas of 1970s housing blocks. He describes instead a city in the midst of vines and dense thickets with a multitude of plant life: a city in wilderness, not a city of lawns—a commingling of the urban and natural worlds that has intriguing possibilities again for us today.

Le Corbusier's well known fascination with fitness and sports is also balanced with a strident and coherent argument for urban farming. In many ways, the urban farm is the holy grail of sustainable cities, providing both greenspace and places for community interaction combined with locally grown food. While farming is a major component of many of the forty-nine cities (from Fourier's Phalanstère to Wright's Broadacre City), few of them bring agriculture within the urban realm. Le Corbusier however proposes 150-square-meter "kitchen gardens" for each resident joined to create communal gardens, equipped with automatic watering and overseen by a resident farmer for every 100 plots. Every day after sports comes the time for farming, an important aspect of the Radiant City often overlooked.

This closer rereading of just one of the forty-nine cities reveals the wealth of information and inspiration to be gleaned from the history of visionary planning. Every city has its forgotten story—with a clarity of vision that seems breathtakingly fresh today—ready to be redis- covered. *49 Cities* is a call to re-engage cities as the site of radical thinking and experimentation moving beyond "green building" towards an embrace of ideas, scale, vision, and common sense combined with unbridled imagination in the pursuit of empowering questioning and reinvention.

49 CITIES IN CHRONOLOGICAL ORDER

ROMAN CITY

Roman Empire, 500 B.C.–500 A.D.
Unknown

Total Site Area (2-D; in m²)	1,493,168

Total Greenspace (m²)	1,029,135
Area: Greenspace: agriculture	1,007,394
Area: Greenspace: lawn	0
Area: Greenspace: park	21,741
Area: Greenspace: wilderness	0

Area of Water (m²)	1,484
Area of Infrastructure (m²)	166,874

Total Built Area [footprint; m²)]	295,675
Area: Housing (footprint)	269,064
Area: Industrial (footprint)	0
Area: Public (footprint)	26,611

Total Population	50,000
Total number housing units	14,286
Number of people per housing unit	3.50

Total Area (3-D; in m²)	2,401,680
Number of Floors: Housing	4
Number of Floors: Industrial	0
Number of Floors: Public	1
Area: Total Built	1,204,116
Area: Housing (3-D)	1,166,932
Area: Industrial (3-D)	0
Area: Public (3-D)	37,255
Area: Open Space (Greenspace + Water + Infrastructure) (3-D)	1,197,493

FAR: 3-D Area / 2-D Area (x)	1.61

DENSITY: total population / site area (2-D) (people per km²)	33,486
DENSITY: total population / total area (3-D) (people per km²)	20,819

2-D Percentages		
Greenspace		69%
Agriculture	67%	
Lawn	1%	
Park	1%	
Wilderness	0%	
Water		0%
Infrastructure		11%
Built Area		20%
Housing	18%	
Industrial	0%	
Public	2%	
Total % of land use (can exceed 100%)		100%

3-D Percentages		
Greenspace		43%
Agriculture	42%	
Lawn	0%	
Park	1%	
Wilderness	0%	
Water		0%
Infrastructure		7%
Built Area		50%
Housing	49%	
Industrial	0%	
Public	1%	
Total % of land use		100%

The Roman City, developed over centuries throughout the Roman Empire as an outpost of colonial rule, was ideally a walled settlement. Established initially with north-south and east-west axial streets, known as the *cardo* and *decamanus*, the city was laid out as a grid, with soldiers' tents giving way to more permanent structures along the streets over time. Each block, or *insula*, was envisioned as a programmable slot and was mixed-use, containing apartments, houses, shops, and workshops, creating a dense city core surrounded by the wall. Between the urbanized zone and city wall was the *pomerium*, a buffer zone, and beyond the wall lay agricultural lands. Urban amenities such as plumbing, reservoirs, drainage and sewers, pedestrian sidewalks, and traffic-calming measures were employed throughout the city, along with public amenities like markets, public baths and toilets, theaters, and religious and governmental buildings.

2D DENSITY RANKING	FAR RANKING	GREENSPACE RANKING	POPULATION RANKING	3D DENSITY RANKING
10/49	25/49	20/49	23/49	8/49

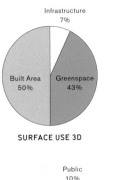

SURFACE USE 3D

LAND USE 2D

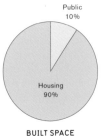

BUILT SPACE

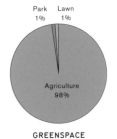

GREENSPACE

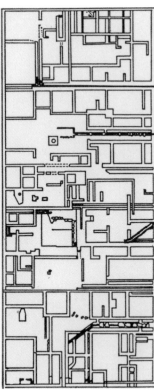

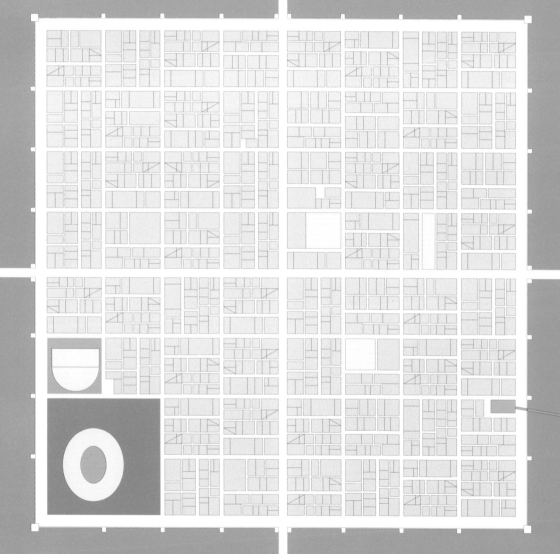

1 mm = 5 m ■■■■■■ 250 m

Total Site Area (2-D; in m²)	8,074,506
Total Greenspace (m²)	5,638,472
Area: Greenspace: agriculture	5,638,472
Area: Greenspace: lawn	0
Area: Greenspace: park	0
Area: Greenspace: wilderness	0
Area of Water (m²)	0
Area of Infrastructure (m²)	460,525
Total Built Area [footprint; m²)]	1,975,509
Area: Housing (footprint)	1,580,407
Area: Industrial (footprint)	0
Area: Public (footprint)	395,102
Total Population	225,000
Total number housing units	64,286
Number of people per housing unit	3.50
Total Area (3-D; in m²)	13,210,830
Number of Floors: Housing	4
Number of Floors: Industrial	0
Number of Floors: Public	2
Area: Total Built	7,111,832
Area: Housing (3-D)	6,321,629
Area: Industrial (3-D)	0
Area: Public (3-D)	790,204
Area: Open Space (Greenspace + Water + Infrastructure) (3-D)	6,098,997
FAR: 3-D Area / 2-D Area (x)	1.64
DENSITY: total population / site area (2-D) (people per km²)	27,865
DENSITY: total population / total area (3-D) (people per km²)	17,031

2-D Percentages		
Greenspace		70%
Agriculture	70%	
Lawn	0%	
Park	0%	
Wilderness	0%	
Water		0%
Infrastructure		6%
Built Area		24%
Housing	20%	
Industrial	0%	
Public	4%	
Total % of land use (can exceed 100%)		100%

3-D Percentages		
Greenspace		43%
Agriculture	43%	
Lawn	0%	
Park	0%	
Wilderness	0%	
Water		0%
Infrastructure		3%
Built Area		54%
Housing	48%	
Industrial	0%	
Public	6%	
Total % of land use		100%

In colonizing the New World, the Spanish conquistadores revived Roman models of town planning to effectively create order in their new settlements. A typical Latin American city was based on a checkerboard plan with a Plaza Mayor surrounded by a cathedral, municipal building, post office, central governmental offices, bank, and a main hotel. Beyond, colonists' housing occupied the blocks. Polluting industries such as tanneries and slaughterhouses were relegated to the outskirts of the city, along with settlements of the Native Americans, upon whose labor the city depended on for construction.

2D DENSITY RANKING	FAR RANKING	GREENSPACE RANKING	POPULATION RANKING	3D DENSITY RANKING
11/49	24/49	18/49	15/49	10/49

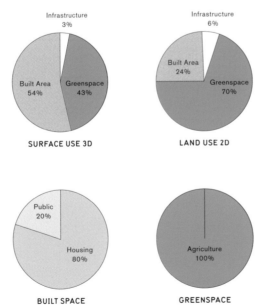

SURFACE USE 3D — Infrastructure 3%, Built Area 54%, Greenspace 43%

LAND USE 2D — Infrastructure 6%, Built Area 24%, Greenspace 70%

BUILT SPACE — Public 20%, Housing 80%

GREENSPACE — Agriculture 100%

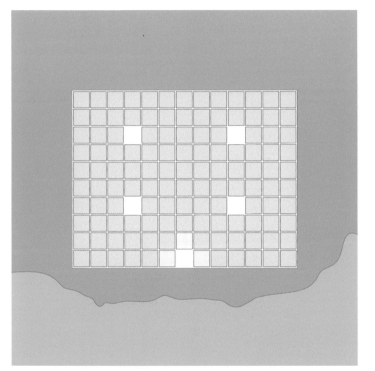

NEUF-BRISACH

France, 1700
Vauban

Total Site Area (2-D; in m²)	**877,845**
Total Greenspace (m²)	**186,492**
Area: Greenspace: agriculture	-
Area: Greenspace: lawn	186,492
Area: Greenspace: park	-
Area: Greenspace: wilderness	-
Area of Water (m²)	**19,476**
Area of Infrastructure (m²)	**542,301**
Total Built Area [footprint; m²)]	**129,576**
Area: Housing (footprint)	105,431
Area: Industrial (footprint)	861
Area: Public (footprint)	23,284
Total Population	**2,000**
Total number housing units	100
Number of people per housing unit	5
Total Area (3-D; in m²)	**1,006,560**
Number of Floors: Housing	2
Number of Floors: Industrial	1
Number of Floors: Public	2
Area: Total Built	**258,290**
Area: Housing (3-D)	210,862
Area: Industrial (3-D)	861
Area: Public (3-D)	46,567
Area: Open Space (Greenspace + Water + Infrastructure) (3-D)	748,270
FAR: 3-D Area / 2-D Area (x)	**1.15**
DENSITY: total population / site area (2-D) (people per km²)	**2,278**
DENSITY: total population / total area (3-D) (people per km²)	**1,987**

Neuf Brisach was one of a number of fortified settlements designed by the French military engineer Vauban. Commissioned as a fortress, the star-shaped complex of walls and ditches enclosed a rectilinear street-grid of houses, public buildings, and markets.

	2D DENSITY RANKING	FAR RANKING	GREENSPACE RANKING	POPULATION RANKING	3D DENSITY RANKING
	39/49	**36/49**	**37/49**	**43/49**	**36/49**

2-D Percentages		
Greenspace		21%
Agriculture	0%	
Lawn	21%	
Park	0%	
Wilderness	0%	
Water		2%
Infrastructure		62%
Built Area		15%
Housing	12%	
Industrial	0%	
Public	3%	
Total % of land use (can exceed 100%)		100%

3-D Percentages		
Greenspace		19%
Agriculture	0%	
Lawn	19%	
Park	0%	
Wilderness	0%	
Water		2%
Infrastructure		53%
Built Area		26%
Housing	21%	
Industrial	0%	
Public	5%	
Total % of land use		100%

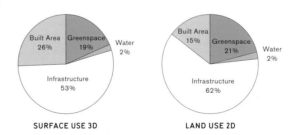

SURFACE USE 3D

Built Area 26%, Greenspace 19%, Water 2%, Infrastructure 53%

LAND USE 2D

Built Area 15%, Greenspace 21%, Water 2%, Infrastructure 62%

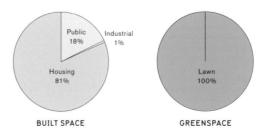

BUILT SPACE

Public 18%, Industrial 1%, Housing 81%

GREENSPACE

Lawn 100%

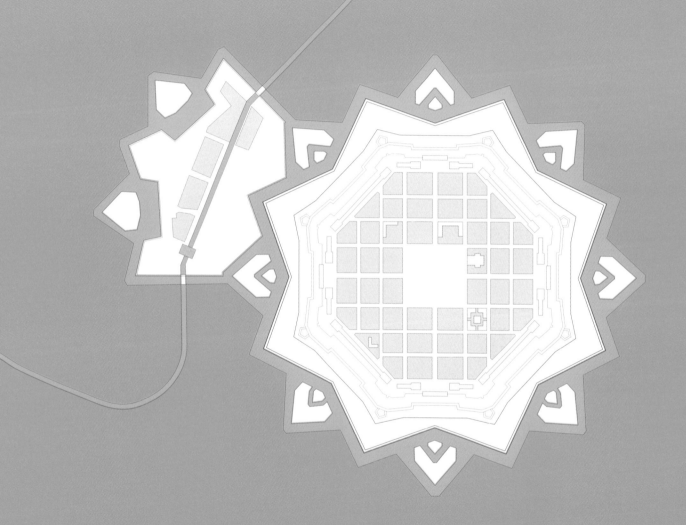

1 mm = 9 m ■■■■■■■ 450 m

SAVANNAH

Total Site Area (2-D; in m²)	4,099,585

Total Greenspace (m²)	1,145,981
Area: Greenspace: agriculture	-
Area: Greenspace: lawn	559,459
Area: Greenspace: park	586,522
Area: Greenspace: wilderness	-

Area of Water (m²)	640,447
Area of Infrastructure (m²)	1,606,174

Total Built Area [footprint; m²)]	706,983
Area: Housing (footprint)	656,748
Area: Industrial (footprint)	20,709
Area: Public (footprint)	29,526

Total Population	30,000
Total number housing units	
Number of people per housing unit	

Total Area (3-D; in m²)	5,463,316
Number of Floors: Housing	3
Number of Floors: Industrial	2
Number of Floors: Public	2
Area: Total Built	2,070,714
Area: Housing (3-D)	1,970,244
Area: Industrial (3-D)	41,418
Area: Public (3-D)	59,052
Area: Open Space (Greenspace + Water + Infrastructure) (3-D)	3,392,602

FAR: 3-D Area / 2-D Area (x)	1.33

DENSITY: total population / site area (2-D) (people per km²)	7,318
DENSITY: total population / total area (3-D) (people per km²)	5,491

2-D Percentages		
Greenspace		28%
Agriculture	0%	
Lawn	14%	
Park	14%	
Wilderness	0%	
Water		16%
Infrastructure		39%
Built Area		17%
Housing	15%	
Industrial	1%	
Public	1%	
Total % of land use (can exceed 100%)		100%

3-D Percentages		
Greenspace		21%
Agriculture	0%	
Lawn	10%	
Park	11%	
Wilderness	0%	
Water		12%
Infrastructure		29%
Built Area		38%
Housing	36%	
Industrial	1%	
Public	1%	
Total % of land use		100%

John Oglethorpe's 1733 plan for Savannah, Georgia, is based on the replication of an urban unit. This unit consists of several blocks of housing surrounding a small green square or park. These quadrants are separated by wider through-streets, and in turn, the blocks within them have narrow local streets. Savannah grew from 1733 to the Civil War by adding these quadrants, and the core of the city retains this structure, interjecting a stately network of greenspaces and a leisurely traffic flow throughout the city.

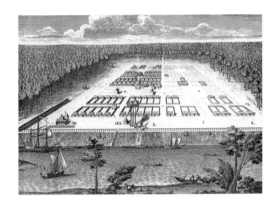

2D DENSITY RANKING	FAR RANKING	GREENSPACE RANKING	POPULATION RANKING	3D DENSITY RANKING
22/49	32/49	33/49	30/49	17/49

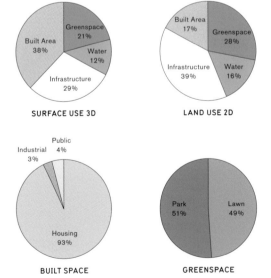

SURFACE USE 3D

LAND USE 2D

BUILT SPACE

GREENSPACE

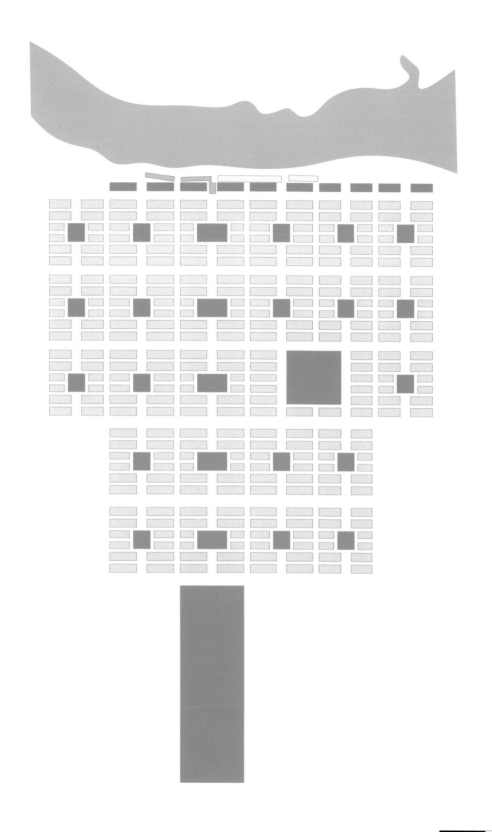

1 mm = 35 m   875 m   1750 m

Arc-et-Senans, France, 1775
Claude-Nicolas Ledoux

Total Site Area (2-D; in m²)	752,781

Total Greenspace (m²)	526,077
Area: Greenspace: agriculture	416,529
Area: Greenspace: lawn	29,951
Area: Greenspace: park	79,597
Area: Greenspace: wilderness	0

Area of Water (m²)	0
Area of Infrastructure (m²)	205,958

Total Built Area [footprint; m²)]	20,746
Area: Housing (footprint)	13,245
Area: Industrial (footprint)	6,682
Area: Public (footprint)	820

Total Population	500
Total number housing units	167
Number of people per housing unit	3.00

Total Area (3-D; in m²)	766,025
Number of Floors: Housing	2
Number of Floors: Industrial	1
Number of Floors: Public	1
Area: Total Built	33,990
Area: Housing (3-D)	26,489
Area: Industrial (3-D)	6,682
Area: Public (3-D)	820
Area: Open Space (Greenspace + Water + Infrastructure) (3-D)	732,035

FAR: 3-D Area / 2-D Area (x)	1.02

DENSITY: total population / site area (2-D) (people per km²)	664
DENSITY: total population / total area (3-D) (people per km²)	653

2-D Percentages		
Greenspace		70%
Agriculture	55%	
Lawn	4%	
Park	11%	
Wilderness	0%	
Water		0%
Infrastructure		27%
Built Area		3%
Housing	2%	
Industrial	1%	
Public	0%	
Total % of land use (can exceed 100%)		100%

3-D Percentages		
Greenspace		69%
Agriculture	54%	
Lawn	5%	
Park	10%	
Wilderness	0%	
Water		0%
Infrastructure		27%
Built Area		4%
Housing	3%	
Industrial	1%	
Public	0%	
Total % of land use		100%

The design of Ledoux's salt works at Chaux was guided by an attempt to rationalize industrial production and to reflect a proto-corporate hierarchy of labor. Informed by Jeremy Bentham's Panopticon, the salt works made a clear attempt to influence the behavior of its occupants: the quarters of the workers were placed in a semi-circle around the main director's building, flanked by industrial buildings. Ostensibly this created an atmosphere of "being watched," fostering obedience in inhabitants.

2D DENSITY RANKING	FAR RANKING	GREENSPACE RANKING	POPULATION RANKING	3D DENSITY RANKING
47/49	47/49	17/49	48/49	46/49

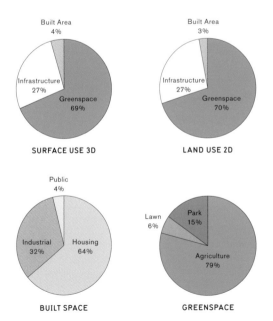

SURFACE USE 3D

Built Area 4%
Infrastructure 27%
Greenspace 69%

LAND USE 2D

Built Area 3%
Infrastructure 27%
Greenspace 70%

BUILT SPACE

Public 4%
Industrial 32%
Housing 64%

GREENSPACE

Lawn 6%
Park 15%
Agriculture 79%

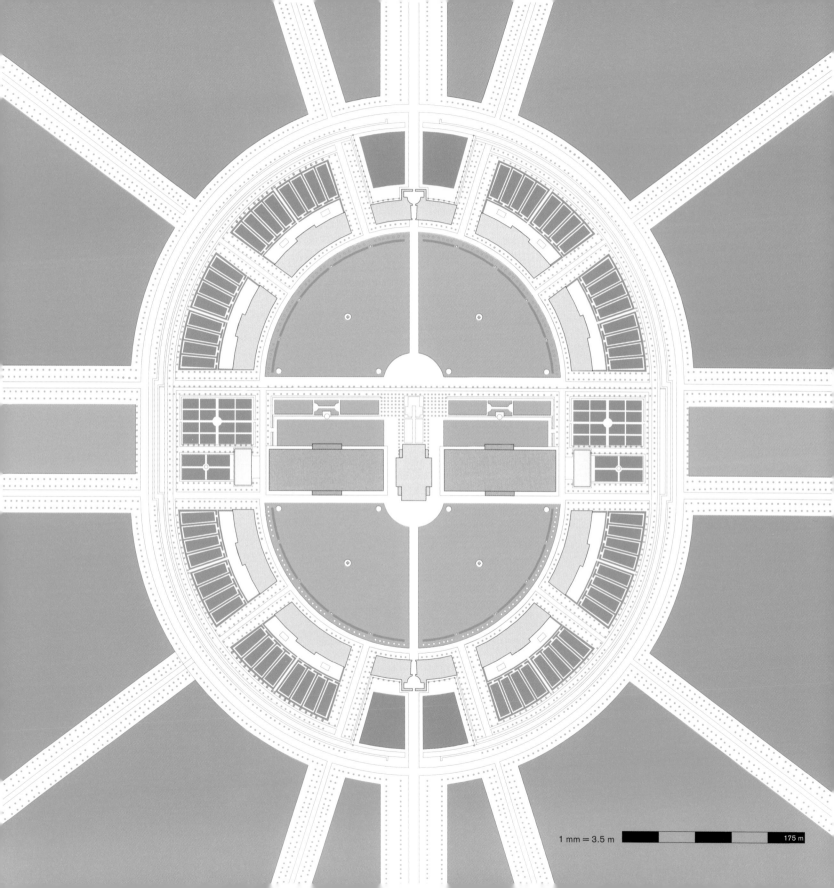

1 mm = 3.5 m 175 m

 PHALANSTÈRE

France, 1800
Charles Fourier

Total Site Area (2-D; in m²)	1,041,089
Total Greenspace (m²)	835,753
Area: Greenspace: agriculture	829,837
Area: Greenspace: lawn	0
Area: Greenspace: park	5,916
Area: Greenspace: wilderness	0
Area of Water (m²)	0
Area of Infrastructure (m²)	69,088
Total Built Area [footprint; m²)]	136,248
Area: Housing (footprint)	86,641
Area: Industrial (footprint)	41,381
Area: Public (footprint)	8,226
Total Population	3,240
Total number housing units	1,080
Number of people per housing unit	3.00
Total Area (3-D; in m²)	1,449,831
Number of Floors: Housing	4
Number of Floors: Industrial	4
Number of Floors: Public	4
Area: Total Built	544,990
Area: Housing (3-D)	346,562
Area: Industrial (3-D)	165,526
Area: Public (3-D)	32,902
Area: Open Space (Greenspace + Water + Infrastructure) (3-D)	904,841
FAR: 3-D Area / 2-D Area (x)	1.39
DENSITY: total population / site area (2-D) (people per km²)	3,112
DENSITY: total population / total area (3-D) (people per km²)	2,235

2-D Percentages		
Greenspace		80%
Agriculture	79%	
Lawn	0%	
Park	1%	
Wilderness	0%	
Water		0%
Infrastructure		7%
Built Area		13%
Housing	8%	
Industrial	4%	
Public	1%	
Total % of land use (can exceed 100%)		100%

3-D Percentages		
Greenspace		57%
Agriculture	57%	
Lawn	0%	
Park	0%	
Wilderness	0%	
Water		0%
Infrastructure		5%
Built Area		38%
Housing	24%	
Industrial	12%	
Public	2%	
Total % of land use		100%

The physical manifestation of Charles Fourier's utopian vision of communal living, the ideal phalanstère, was an all-encompassing living unit for one phalanx of 1,620 people. The phalanx was to be a family-like social structure, supporting free love, rejecting industrialization, and emphasizing manual labor. The four- to six-level complex featured two wings, along with a central portion dedicated to dining, finance, libraries, and worship. The first wing housed all "noisy" activities, such as industrial production and kitchens, while the second wing featured ballrooms and reception halls in addition to the residences. The building was ideally situated on a 5,000-acre agricultural estate, cultivated by the residents. Fourier predicted that there would be six million phalanxes eventually, ruled initially by a world omniarch, and later, a world congress of phalanxes. A phalanx was actually created in New Jersey, in 1843, and remained occupied until 1856, but was much smaller in its physical and social scope than Fourier's ideal colony.

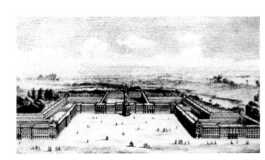

2D DENSITY RANKING	FAR RANKING	GREENSPACE RANKING	POPULATION RANKING	3D DENSITY RANKING
34/49	31/49	13/49	40/49	33/49

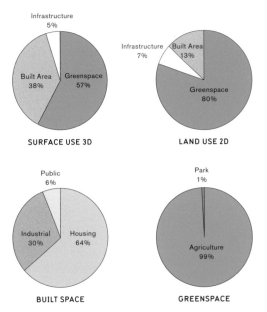

SURFACE USE 3D

LAND USE 2D

BUILT SPACE

GREENSPACE

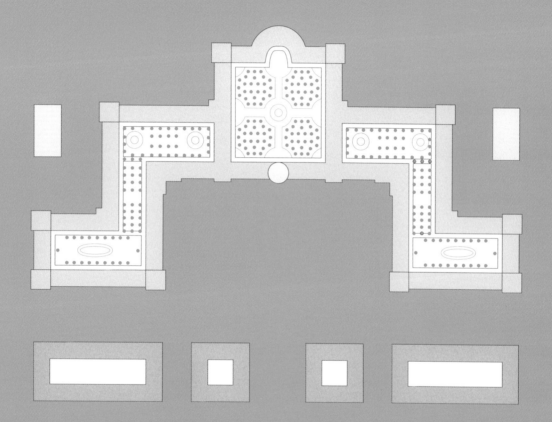

Total Site Area (2-D; in m²)	881,922

Total Greenspace (m²)	277,468
Area: Greenspace: agriculture	
Area: Greenspace: lawn	165,349
Area: Greenspace: park	112,119
Area: Greenspace: wilderness	

Area of Water (m²)	97,312
Area of Infrastructure (m²)	325,087

Total Built Area [footprint; m²)]	182,056
Area: Housing (footprint)	81,504
Area: Industrial (footprint)	
Area: Public (footprint)	100,552

Total Population	2,000
Total number housing units	
Number of people per housing unit	

Total Area (3-D; in m²)	881,922
Number of Floors: Housing	1
Number of Floors: Industrial	1
Number of Floors: Public	1
Area: Total Built	182,056
Area: Housing (3-D)	81,504
Area: Industrial (3-D)	-
Area: Public (3-D)	100,552
Area: Open Space (Greenspace + Water + Infrastructure) (3-D)	699,867

FAR: 3-D Area / 2-D Area (x)	1.00

DENSITY: total population / site area (2-D) (people per km²)	2,268
DENSITY: total population / total area (3-D) (people per km²)	2,268

2-D Percentages		
Greenspace		31%
Agriculture	0%	
Lawn	18%	
Park	13%	
Wilderness	0%	
Water		11%
Infrastructure		37%
Built Area		21%
Housing	9%	
Industrial	0%	
Public	11%	
Total % of land use (can exceed 100%)		100%

3-D Percentages		
Greenspace		31%
Agriculture	0%	
Lawn	18%	
Park	13%	
Wilderness	0%	
Water		11%
Infrastructure		37%
Built Area		21%
Housing	10%	
Industrial	0%	
Public	11%	
Total % of land use		100%

While Thomas Jefferson never formally proposed a precise city plan, Jeffersonville, Indiana, was based on his idea for a checkerboard urban pattern. A rectilinear grid of blocks would alternate between housing and park squares, providing green frontage to all residents. This green-centered urban plan was an early reaction to the "pestilences" and "miasmas" of the city, an idea replicated in many later schemes, such as the Garden City and Radiant City.

2D DENSITY RANKING	FAR RANKING	GREENSPACE RANKING	POPULATION RANKING	3D DENSITY RANKING
40/49	48/49	32/49	41/49	32/49

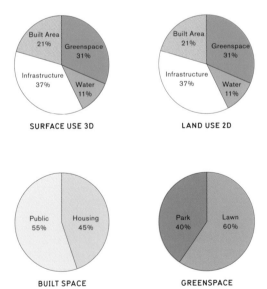

SURFACE USE 3D

LAND USE 2D

BUILT SPACE

GREENSPACE

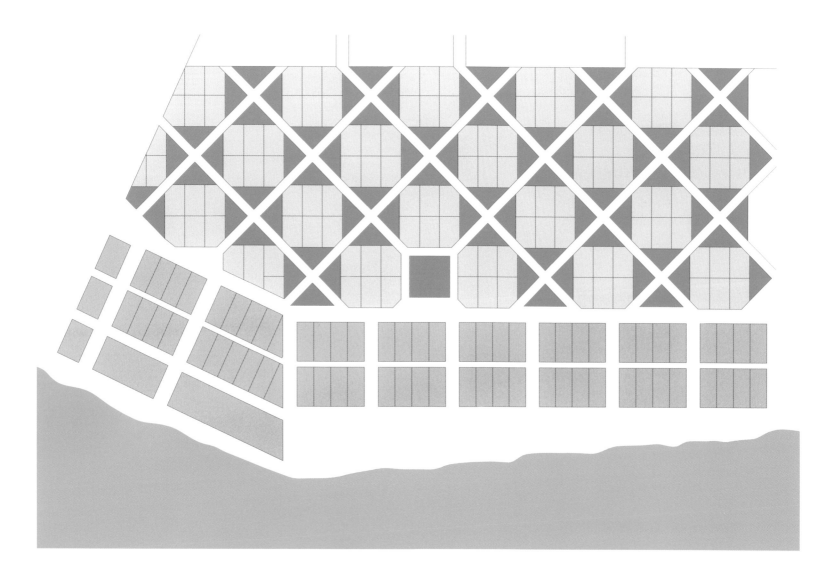

1 mm = 6 m ▮▮▮▮ 300 m

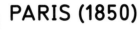 # PARIS (1850)

France, 1850
George-Eugène Haussmann

Total Site Area (2-D; in m²)	**106,572,889**
Total Greenspace (m²)	**25,240,246**
Area: Greenspace: agriculture	0
Area: Greenspace: lawn	4,988,322
Area: Greenspace: park	20,251,924
Area: Greenspace: wilderness	0
Area of Water (m²)	**2,445,801**
Area of Infrastructure (m²)	**12,613,418**
Total Built Area [footprint; m²)]	**66,273,424**
Area: Housing (footprint)	37,775,852
Area: Industrial (footprint)	9,941,014
Area: Public (footprint)	18,556,559
Total Population	**1,500,000**
Total number housing units	500,000
Number of people per housing unit	3.00
Total Area (3-D; in m²)	**321,496,940**
Number of Floors: Housing	6
Number of Floors: Industrial	1
Number of Floors: Public	3
Area: Total Built	**281,197,475**
Area: Housing (3-D)	215,586,786
Area: Industrial (3-D)	9,941,014
Area: Public (3-D)	55,669,676
Area: Open Space (Greenspace + Water + Infrastructure) (3-D)	40,299,465
FAR: 3-D Area / 2-D Area (x)	**3.02**
DENSITY: total population / site area (2-D) (people per km²)	**14,075**
DENSITY: total population / total area (3-D) (people per km²)	**4,667**

2-D Percentages	
Greenspace	**24%**
Agriculture	0%
Lawn	5%
Park	19%
Wilderness	0%
Water	**2%**
Infrastructure	**12%**
Built Area	**62%**
Housing	36%
Industrial	9%
Public	17%
Total % of land use (can exceed 100%)	**100%**

3-D Percentages	
Greenspace	**8%**
Agriculture	0%
Lawn	2%
Park	6%
Wilderness	0%
Water	**1%**
Infrastructure	**4%**
Built Area	**87%**
Housing	75%
Industrial	3%
Public	9%
Total % of land use	**100%**

Haussmann's modernization of Paris through the creation of a network of wide boulevards essentially shaped today's city. Prior to the rule of Napoleon III, Paris was primarily made up of a dense and irregular street grid without the axial boulevards found in Enlightenment-era cities, like nearby Versailles. In an attempt to "ease" circulation, Haussmann superimposed a number of interconnected incisions on the urban land-scape. This system of boulevards also included various aesthetic and infrastructural guidelines, imposing height zoning and material specifi-cations for buildings along the new streets. Additionally, it allowed troops to march through the city, and facilitated crowd control by preventing easy construction of barricades. The scale of this urban renovation inspired later plans, both real and proposed, from Le Corbusier's Plan Voisin to Robert Moses' modern car-based interpretations.

2D DENSITY RANKING	FAR RANKING	GREENSPACE RANKING	POPULATION RANKING	3D DENSITY RANKING
19/49	10/49	35/49	7/49	20/49

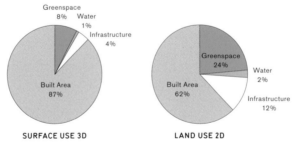

SURFACE USE 3D — Greenspace 8%, Water 1%, Infrastructure 4%, Built Area 87%

LAND USE 2D — Greenspace 24%, Water 2%, Infrastructure 12%, Built Area 62%

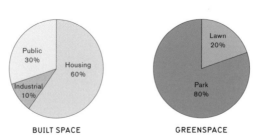

BUILT SPACE — Public 30%, Housing 60%, Industrial 10%

GREENSPACE — Lawn 20%, Park 80%

1 mm = 60 m |███ 1 km ███| |███ 3 km|

Austria, 1890
Camillo Sitte

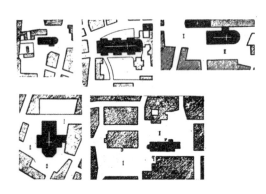

Camillo Sitte's unrealized master plan for this community in Silesia was based on many of the guidelines he established in *City Planning According to Artistic Principles*, his study of admirable aspects of medieval cities throughout Europe. The small residential city was comprised of an irregular street grid, interspersed with a knot-like network of public squares of varying sizes. Larger squares were to be anchored by public buildings or churches, and a series of parks would be embedded throughout the city.

Total Site Area (2-D; in m²)	1,643,847
Total Greenspace (m²)	832,706
Area: Greenspace: agriculture	393,802
Area: Greenspace: lawn	324,154
Area: Greenspace: park	114,751
Area: Greenspace: wilderness	
Area of Water (m²)	-
Area of Infrastructure (m²)	264,555
Total Built Area [footprint; m²)]	546,586
Area: Housing (footprint)	539,858
Area: Industrial (footprint)	-
Area: Public (footprint)	6,728
Total Population	6,000
Total number housing units	
Number of people per housing unit	
Total Area (3-D; in m²)	2,730,290
Number of Floors: Housing	3
Number of Floors: Industrial	1
Number of Floors: Public	2
Area: Total Built	1,633,029
Area: Housing (3-D)	1,619,574
Area: Industrial (3-D)	-
Area: Public (3-D)	13,455
Area: Open Space (Greenspace + Water + Infrastructure) (3-D)	1,097,261
FAR: 3-D Area / 2-D Area (x)	1.66
DENSITY: total population / site area (2-D) (people per km²)	3,650
DENSITY: total population / total area (3-D) (people per km²)	2,198

2-D Percentages		
Greenspace		51%
Agriculture	24%	
Lawn	20%	
Park	7%	
Wilderness	0%	
Water		0%
Infrastructure		16%
Built Area		33%
Housing	32%	
Industrial	0%	
Public	1%	
Total % of land use (can exceed 100%)		100%

3-D Percentages		
Greenspace		30%
Agriculture	14%	
Lawn	12%	
Park	4%	
Wilderness	0%	
Water		0%
Infrastructure		10%
Built Area		60%
Housing	60%	
Industrial	0%	
Public	0%	
Total % of land use		100%

2D DENSITY RANKING	FAR RANKING	GREENSPACE RANKING	POPULATION RANKING	3D DENSITY RANKING
33/49	23/49	26/49	38/49	34/49

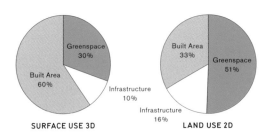

SURFACE USE 3D
Greenspace 30%
Built Area 60%
Infrastructure 10%

LAND USE 2D
Built Area 33%
Greenspace 51%
Infrastructure 16%

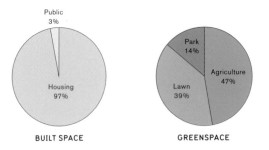

BUILT SPACE
Public 3%
Housing 97%

GREENSPACE
Park 14%
Agriculture 47%
Lawn 39%

1 mm = 8 m ▮▮▮▮▮□□□▮▮▮□□□▮▮▮ 400 m

Total Site Area (2-D; in m²)	**5,856,402**
Total Greenspace (m²)	**3,600,589**
Area: Greenspace: agriculture	1,038,888
Area: Greenspace: lawn	1,458,459
Area: Greenspace: park	1,103,242
Area: Greenspace: wilderness	-
Area of Water (m²)	**-**
Area of Infrastructure (m²)	**1,264,102**
Total Built Area [footprint; m²)]	**991,712**
Area: Housing (footprint)	298,721
Area: Industrial (footprint)	526,772
Area: Public (footprint)	166,219
Total Population	**32,000**
Total number housing units	8,000
Number of people per housing unit	4
Total Area (3-D; in m²)	**6,848,114**
Number of Floors: Housing	2
Number of Floors: Industrial	2
Number of Floors: Public	2
Area: Total Built	**1,983,423**
Area: Housing (3-D)	597,441
Area: Industrial (3-D)	1,053,544
Area: Public (3-D)	332,438
Area: Open Space (Greenspace + Water + Infrastructure) (3-D)	4,864,691
FAR: 3-D Area / 2-D Area (x)	**1.17**
DENSITY: total population / site area (2-D) (people per km²)	**5,464**
DENSITY: total population / total area (3-D) (people per km²)	**4,673**

2-D Percentages		
Greenspace		**61%**
	Agriculture	18%
	Lawn	25%
	Park	18%
	Wilderness	0%
Water		**0%**
Infrastructure		**22%**
Built Area		**17%**
	Housing	5%
	Industrial	9%
	Public	3%
Total % of land use (can exceed 100%)		**100%**

3-D Percentages		
Greenspace		**53%**
	Agriculture	16%
	Lawn	21%
	Park	16%
	Wilderness	0%
Water		**0%**
Infrastructure		**18%**
Built Area		**29%**
	Housing	9%
	Industrial	15%
	Public	5%
Total % of land use		**100%**

The Garden City sought to combine the best aspects of country and city life with a comprehensive social vision for a hybrid place Howard called the "town-country." The Garden City was composed of a 6,000-acre estate, with 1,000 acres for the city itself, 265 acres for parkland, and the rest reserved for agriculture. Concentric rings of program and parkland create the plan of the city. The center features administrative buildings, flanked by a Central Park, which is surrounded by a "Crystal Palace," an all-weather shopping arcade. Further toward the periphery, blocks of housing straddle axial and circular avenues. A park-like Grand Avenue contains schools and religious buildings. Industries are situated with easy access to a peripheral railway that connects the city to other Garden Cities. The city is surrounded by an agricultural green-belt. In subsequent settlements, this zone is kept intact around each new city.

2D DENSITY RANKING	FAR RANKING	GREENSPACE RANKING	POPULATION RANKING	3D DENSITY RANKING
26/49	34/49	24/49	27/49	19/49

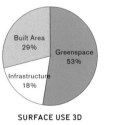

SURFACE USE 3D

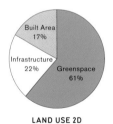

LAND USE 2D

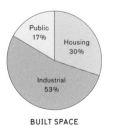

BUILT SPACE

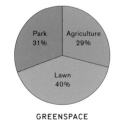

GREENSPACE

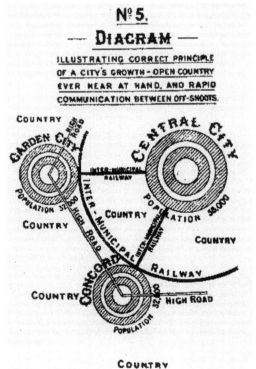

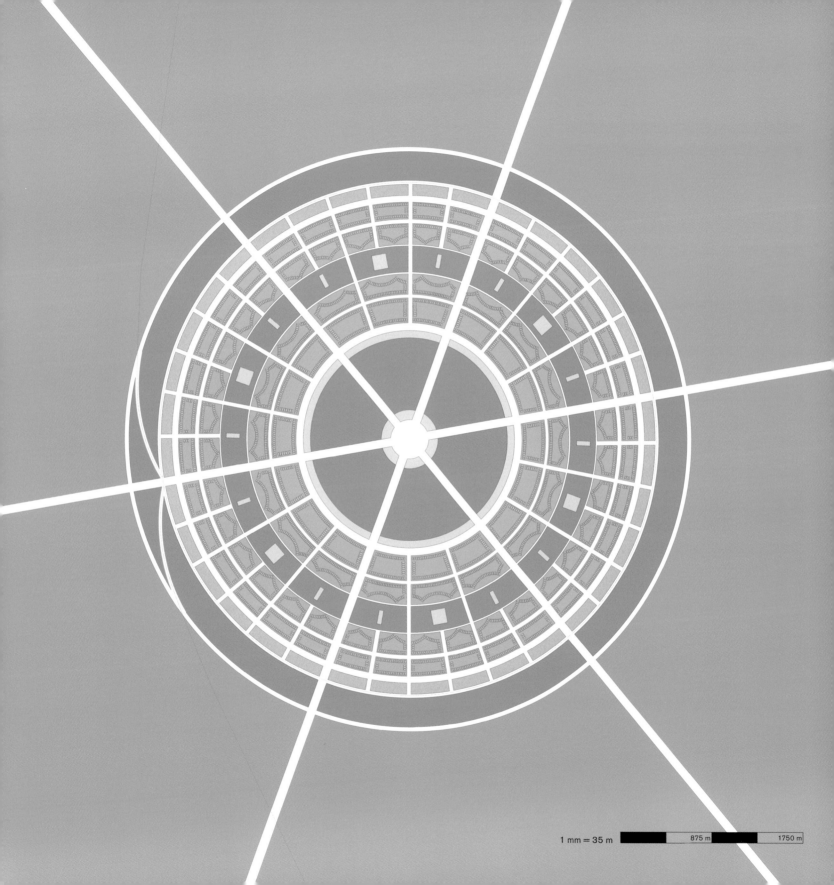

1 mm = 35 m

875 m   1750 m

Total Site Area (2-D; in m²)	1,000,000

Total Greenspace (m²)	990,868
Area: Greenspace: agriculture	929,819
Area: Greenspace: lawn	61,049
Area: Greenspace: park	
Area: Greenspace: wilderness	

Area of Water (m²)	-
Area of Infrastructure (m²)	4,267

Total Built Area [footprint; m²)]	10,843
Area: Housing (footprint)	9,144
Area: Industrial (footprint)	
Area: Public (footprint)	1,699

Total Population	1,000
Total number housing units	
Number of people per housing unit	

Total Area (3-D; in m²)	1,027,664
Number of Floors: Housing	3
Number of Floors: Industrial	3
Number of Floors: Public	3
Area: Total Built	32,528
Area: Housing (3-D)	27,432
Area: Industrial (3-D)	-
Area: Public (3-D)	5,096
Area: Open Space (Greenspace + Water + Infrastructure) (3-D)	995,135

FAR: 3-D Area / 2-D Area (x)	1.03

DENSITY: total population / site area (2-D) (people per km²)	1,000
DENSITY: total population / total area (3-D) (people per km²)	973

2-D Percentages		
Greenspace		99%
	Agriculture	93%
	Lawn	6%
	Park	0%
	Wilderness	0%
Water		0%
Infrastructure		1%
Built Area		1%
	Housing	1%
	Industrial	0%
	Public	0%
Total % of land use (can exceed 100%)		101%

3-D Percentages		
Greenspace		96%
	Agriculture	90%
	Lawn	6%
	Park	0%
	Wilderness	0%
Water		0%
Infrastructure		1%
Built Area		3%
	Housing	3%
	Industrial	0%
	Public	0%
Total % of land use		100%

Edgar Chambless's Roadtown, proposed in 1910 and reconfigured in 1931, was one of the first linear-city schemes, incorporating transit lines, infrastructure, and buildings for all functions. Roadtown was proposed to connect Baltimore and Washington with a continuous development. This building-city was to have rail lines at multiple subterranean levels and row houses above. The top surface of the row houses would be a drivable roadway, and the whole complex would be interspersed with public and commercial buildings. Residents would also have access to agricultural plots directly adjacent to their houses and extending several hundred feet into the countryside.

2D DENSITY RANKING	FAR RANKING	GREENSPACE RANKING	POPULATION RANKING	3D DENSITY RANKING
45/49	46/49	3/49	46/49	41/49

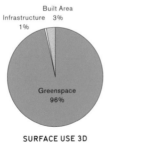

SURFACE USE 3D

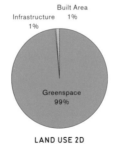

LAND USE 2D

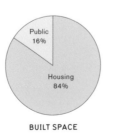

BUILT SPACE

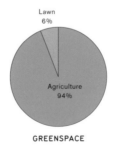

GREENSPACE

1 mm = 5 m   250 m

Southeastern France, 1917
Tony Garnier

Total Site Area (2-D; in m²)	14,060,740

Total Greenspace (m²)	3,261,872
Area: Greenspace: agriculture	-
Area: Greenspace: lawn	2,088,660
Area: Greenspace: park	1,173,212
Area: Greenspace: wilderness	-

Area of Water (m²)	-
Area of Infrastructure (m²)	2,721,516

Total Built Area [footprint; m²)]	8,077,351
Area: Housing (footprint)	2,451,906
Area: Industrial (footprint)	5,332,607
Area: Public (footprint)	292,839

Total Population	36,000
Total number housing units	9,000
Number of people per housing unit	4

Total Area (3-D; in m²)	22,138,091
Number of Floors: Housing	2
Number of Floors: Industrial	2
Number of Floors: Public	2
Area: Total Built	16,154,703
Area: Housing (3-D)	4,903,812
Area: Industrial (3-D)	10,665,213
Area: Public (3-D)	585,678
Area: Open Space (Greenspace + Water + Infrastructure) (3-D)	5,983,388

FAR: 3-D Area / 2-D Area (x)	1.57

DENSITY: total population / site area (2-D) (people per km²)	2,560
DENSITY: total population / total area (3-D) (people per km²)	1,626

2-D Percentages		
Greenspace		23%
Agriculture	0%	
Lawn	15%	
Park	8%	
Wilderness	0%	
Water		0%
Infrastructure		19%
Built Area		58%
Housing	18%	
Industrial	38%	
Public	2%	
Total % of land use (can exceed 100%)		100%

3-D Percentages		
Greenspace		15%
Agriculture	0%	
Lawn	9%	
Park	6%	
Wilderness	0%	
Water		0%
Infrastructure		12%
Built Area		73%
Housing	22%	
Industrial	48%	
Public	3%	
Total % of land use		100%

Tony Garnier's plan for a hypothetical industrial city to be located in southeastern France was a vividly detailed attempt to create a realistic, reachable urban ideal. The city, with needs similar to those of regional cities like St. Etienne, would have "proximity to raw materials, the existence of a natural energy source easily harnessed for industry, and convenience of modes of transportation." With these goals in mind, Garnier designed the Cité Industrielle on a plateau above a floodplain, with a large metallurgical plant situated on the river below. The plan separates residential, commercial, and industrial zones. The plateau zone incorporates the residential, administrative and public functions. Mines, agribusiness, a hydroelectric dam, and other industry is removed from the urban core; hospitals and sanatoriums are situated at elevations higher than the bulk of the city. Soon after presenting his plans, Garnier began building public works extensively in Lyon.

2D DENSITY RANKING	FAR RANKING	GREENSPACE RANKING	POPULATION RANKING	3D DENSITY RANKING
36/49	27/49	36/49	26/49	38/49

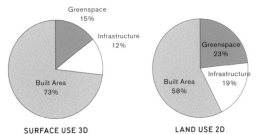

SURFACE USE 3D

LAND USE 2D

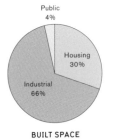

BUILT SPACE

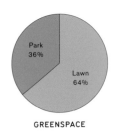

GREENSPACE

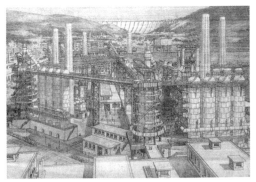

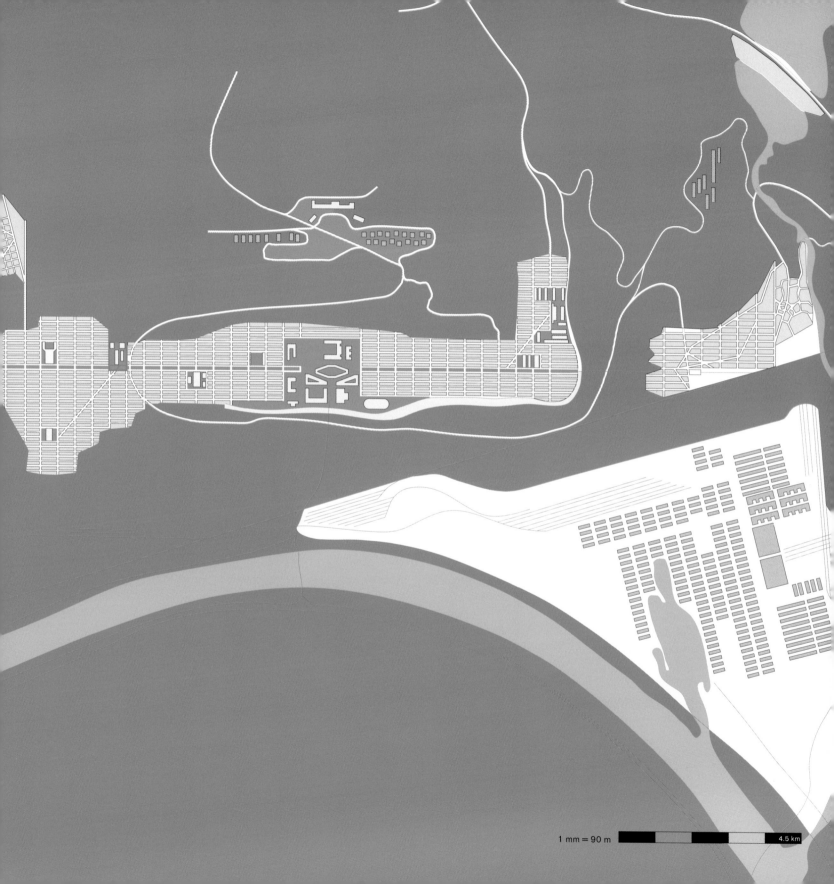

1 mm = 90 m   4.5 km

Total Site Area (2-D; in m²)	**4,018,591**
Total Greenspace (m²)	**1,902,899**
Area: Greenspace: agriculture	-
Area: Greenspace: lawn	1,194,010
Area: Greenspace: park	708,889
Area: Greenspace: wilderness	-
Area of Water (m²)	**69,622**
Area of Infrastructure (m²)	**1,460,900**
Total Built Area [footprint; m²)]	**654,792**
Area: Housing (footprint)	480,193
Area: Industrial (footprint)	24,106
Area: Public (footprint)	150,493
Total Population	**22,040**
Total number housing units	1,500
Number of people per housing unit	19
Total Area (3-D; in m²)	**6,401,786**
Number of Floors: Housing	4
Number of Floors: Industrial	6
Number of Floors: Public	6
Area: Total Built	**2,968,364**
Area: Housing (3-D)	1,920,770
Area: Industrial (3-D)	144,639
Area: Public (3-D)	902,956
Area: Open Space (Greenspace + Water + Infrastructure) (3-D)	3,433,422
FAR: 3-D Area / 2-D Area (x)	**1.59**
DENSITY: total population / site area (2-D) (people per km²)	**5,485**
DENSITY: total population / total area (3-D) (people per km²)	**3,443**

2-D Percentages	
Greenspace	**48%**
Agriculture	0%
Lawn	30%
Park	18%
Wilderness	0%
Water	**2%**
Infrastructure	**36%**
Built Area	**16%**
Housing	11%
Industrial	1%
Public	4%
Total % of land use (can exceed 100%)	**102%**

3-D Percentages	
Greenspace	**30%**
Agriculture	0%
Lawn	19%
Park	11%
Wilderness	0%
Water	**1%**
Infrastructure	**23%**
Built Area	**46%**
Housing	30%
Industrial	2%
Public	14%
Total % of land use	**100%**

Richard Neutra's proposal for a Modernist city of circulation, Rush City, was never codified as a singular plan, but was mostly a collection of rules and planning ideas based on reactions to European and American cities. Like Le Corbusier's Radiant City, Rush City aims to create a car-friendly environment of high-rise residential and commercial buildings. A desire for widespread greenery, access to sunlight and air, and ease of automotive circulation led to Neutra's focus on a rational and hierarchical road layout. Discrete parts of the city are designated as industrial, business/commercial, administrative, leisure, multi-family residential blocks, and single-family row houses. The city can grow by adding sectors and roads.

2D DENSITY RANKING	FAR RANKING	GREENSPACE RANKING	POPULATION RANKING	3D DENSITY RANKING
25/49	26/49	28/49	31/49	26/49

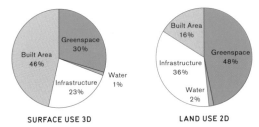

SURFACE USE 3D

LAND USE 2D

BUILT SPACE

GREENSPACE

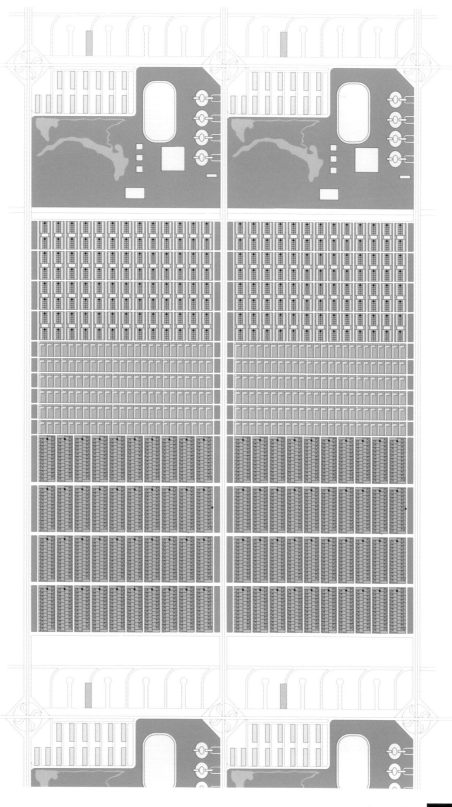

1 mm = 20 m   500 m   1000 m

Total Site Area (2-D; in m²)	**11,390,923**
Total Greenspace (m²)	**9,864,535**
Area: Greenspace: agriculture	6,045,712
Area: Greenspace: lawn	838,433
Area: Greenspace: park	1,565,891
Area: Greenspace: wilderness	1,414,499
Area of Water (m²)	**231,435**
Area of Infrastructure (m²)	**827,610**
Total Built Area [footprint; m²)]	**467,343**
Area: Housing (footprint)	84,729
Area: Industrial (footprint)	64,918
Area: Public (footprint)	317,696
Total Population	**7,000**
Total number housing units	100
Number of people per housing unit	50
Total Area (3-D; in m²)	**11,793,348**
Number of Floors: Housing	2
Number of Floors: Industrial	1
Number of Floors: Public	2
Area: Total Built	**869,768**
Area: Housing (3-D)	169,458
Area: Industrial (3-D)	64,918
Area: Public (3-D)	635,392
Area: Open Space (Greenspace + Water + Infrastructure) (3-D)	10,923,580
FAR: 3-D Area / 2-D Area (x)	**1.04**
DENSITY: total population / site area (2-D) (people per km²)	**615**
DENSITY: total population / total area (3-D) (people per km²)	**594**

2-D Percentages	
Greenspace	**87%**
Agriculture	53%
Lawn	7%
Park	15%
Wilderness	12%
Water	**2%**
Infrastructure	**7%**
Built Area	**4%**
Housing	1%
Industrial	1%
Public	2%
Total % of land use (can exceed 100%)	**100%**

3-D Percentages	
Greenspace	**84%**
Agriculture	52%
Lawn	7%
Park	13%
Wilderness	12%
Water	**2%**
Infrastructure	**7%**
Built Area	**7%**
Housing	1%
Industrial	1%
Public	5%
Total % of land use	**100%**

Broadacre City, Frank Lloyd Wright's total vision for the new American way of living, was driven by Wright's reaction to perceived urban ills of the day. Based on a "Usonian" lifestyle—agrarian, artisan, self-sufficient, and anti-urban—Broadacre dispersed and decentralized the population into the countryside. Broadacre as depicted in Wright's enormous model, constructed in the early 1930s and modified by his students at Taliesin continually for decades, was a sprawling, automobile-based environment, interlaced with small farms, roadside markets, schools, small industry, and public complexes—not unlike postwar American suburbs. Subdivided into one-acre plots, the land was largely cultivated but included "woodplots" that would be held in trust for future Usonians, who would each inherit one acre at birth.

2D DENSITY RANKING	FAR RANKING	GREENSPACE RANKING	POPULATION RANKING	3D DENSITY RANKING
48/49	44/49	10/49	37/49	47/49

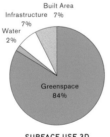

SURFACE USE 3D

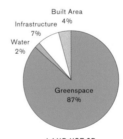

LAND USE 2D

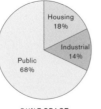

BUILT SPACE

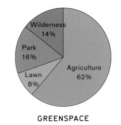

GREENSPACE

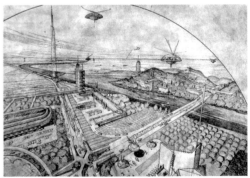

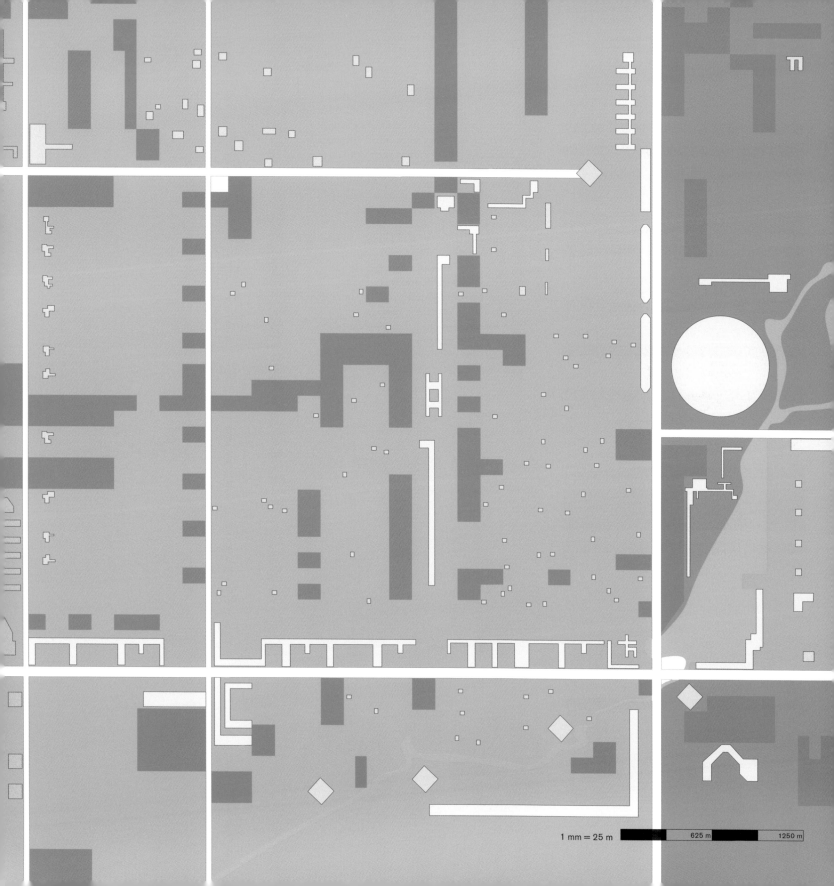

1 mm = 25 m

625 m   1250 m

 **RADIANT CITY**

Global, 1935
Le Corbusier

Total Site Area (2-D; in m²)	**114,290,621**
Total Greenspace (m²)	**114,290,621**
Area: Greenspace: agriculture	0
Area: Greenspace: lawn	0
Area: Greenspace: park	54,689,799
Area: Greenspace: wilderness	59,600,822
Area of Water (m²)	**737,602**
Area of Infrastructure (m²)	**12,854,154**
Total Built Area [footprint; m²)]	**8,479,819**
Area: Housing (footprint)	2,066,675
Area: Industrial (footprint)	5,618,460
Area: Public (footprint)	794,684
Total Population	**2,073,600**
Total number housing units	829,440
Number of people per housing unit	2.50
Total Area (3-D; in m²)	**255,324,701**
Number of Floors: Housing	13
Number of Floors: Industrial	8
Number of Floors: Public	70
Area: Total Built	**127,442,324**
Area: Housing (3-D)	26,866,770
Area: Industrial (3-D)	44,947,684
Area: Public (3-D)	55,627,870
Area: Open Space (Greenspace + Water + Infrastructure) (3-D)	127,882,377
FAR: 3-D Area / 2-D Area (x)	**2.23**
DENSITY: total population / site area (2-D) (people per km²)	**18,143**
DENSITY: total population / total area (3-D) (people per km²)	**8,121**

2-D Percentages	
Greenspace	**100%**
Agriculture	0%
Lawn	0%
Park	48%
Wilderness	52%
Water	**1%**
Infrastructure	**11%**
Built Area	**7%**
Housing	2%
Industrial	4%
Public	1%
Total % of land use (can exceed 100%)	**119%**

3-D Percentages	
Greenspace	**45%**
Agriculture	0%
Lawn	0%
Park	22%
Wilderness	23%
Water	**0%**
Infrastructure	**5%**
Built Area	**50%**
Housing	11%
Industrial	17%
Public	22%
Total % of land use	**100%**

Le Corbusier's Radiant City attempted to open the city to light, air, and nature, while simultaneously achieving extremely high residential densities. The park-like ground plane of the city was completely open to the pedestrian, crisscrossed by elevated highways and dotted with towers on pilotis. Horizontally, the city was zoned into specific areas of residential, administrative/business, and industrial functions. Residents inhabited superblocks, self-contained residential neighborhood buildings of 2,700 residents that had communal amenities and recreational facilities. Cruciform office buildings in the business zone of the city were to be forty-stories tall, housing 3,200 workers per building. The plan was highly influential in residential and commercial planning for decades after it was introduced.

2D DENSITY RANKING	FAR RANKING	GREENSPACE RANKING	POPULATION RANKING	3D DENSITY RANKING
16/49	17/49	1/49*	5/49	15/49

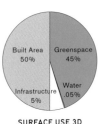

SURFACE USE 3D

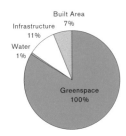

LAND USE 2D

BUILT SPACE

GREENSPACE

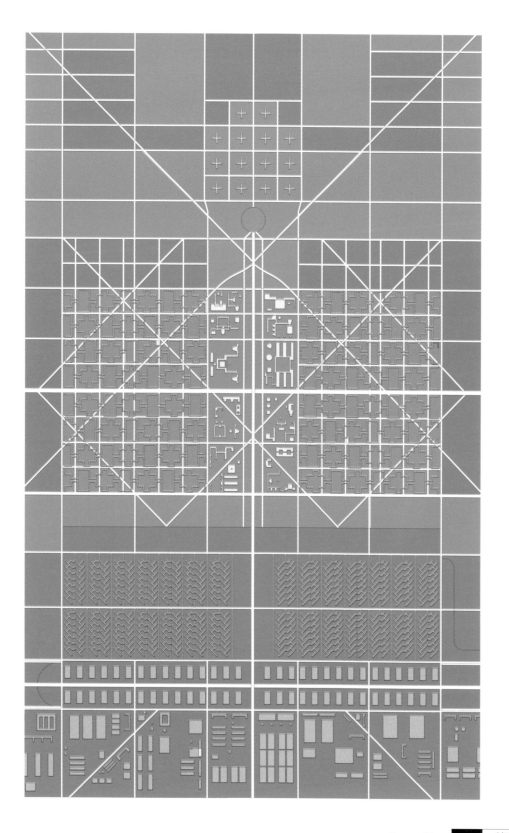

1 mm = 60 m

CHICAGO

Illinois, USA, 1940
Ludwig Hilberseimer

Total Site Area (2-D; in m²)	24,221,432,843

Total Greenspace (m²)	17,621,584,235
Area: Greenspace: agriculture	0
Area: Greenspace: lawn	0
Area: Greenspace: park	92,014,135
Area: Greenspace: wilderness	17,529,570,100

Area of Water (m²)	6,382,102,370
Area of Infrastructure (m²)	166,758,180

Total Built Area [footprint; m²)]	50,988,058
Area: Housing (footprint)	7,781,560
Area: Industrial (footprint)	27,957,424
Area: Public (footprint)	15,249,075

Total Population	4,000,000
Total number housing units	80,808
Number of people per housing unit	49.50

Total Area (3-D; in m²)	24,221,432,843
Number of Floors: Housing	1
Number of Floors: Industrial	1
Number of Floors: Public	1
Area: Total Built	50,988,058
Area: Housing (3-D)	7,781,560
Area: Industrial (3-D)	27,957,424
Area: Public (3-D)	15,249,075
Area: Open Space (Greenspace + Water + Infrastructure) (3-D)	24,170,444,785

FAR: 3-D Area / 2-D Area (x)	1.00

DENSITY: total population / site area (2-D) (people per km²)	165
DENSITY: total population / total area (3-D) (people per km²)	165

2-D Percentages	
Greenspace	73%
Agriculture	0%
Lawn	0%
Park	1%
Wilderness	72%
Water	26%
Infrastructure	1%
Built Area	0%
Housing	0%
Industrial	0%
Public	0%
Total % of land use (can exceed 100%)	100%

3-D Percentages	
Greenspace	73%
Agriculture	0%
Lawn	0%
Park	1%
Wilderness	72%
Water	26%
Infrastructure	1%
Built Area	0%
Housing	0%
Industrial	0%
Public	0%
Total % of land use	100%

Ludwig Hilberseimer, working largely in the shadow of Mies van der Rohe, first in Germany and later in Chicago, proposed a number of conceptual, regional-scale projects, in line with Modernist reactions to the industrialized city. His scheme for decentralizing the Chicago area relies on a separation of industry from residential, cultural and white-collar work areas, based equally on a fear of nuclear warfare and on wind patterns' ability to disperse air pollution. The Chicago plan consists of a gridded road network with cul-de-sac residential/commercial modules dispersed over hundreds of square miles. Hilberseimer's work was almost entirely devoid of form at the scale of the building—the destruction and dispersal of the old city was purely technical. His vision of the dispersed, cul-de-sac model for future residential communities, however, proved to be prophetic.

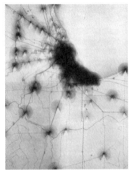 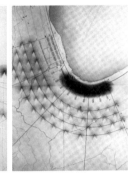

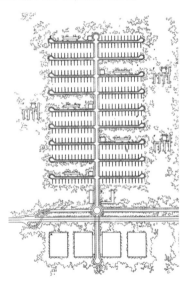

2D DENSITY RANKING	FAR RANKING	GREENSPACE RANKING	POPULATION RANKING	3D DENSITY RANKING
49/49	49/49	16/49	4/49	49/49

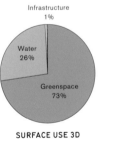

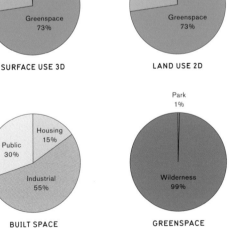

SURFACE USE 3D

LAND USE 2D

BUILT SPACE

GREENSPACE

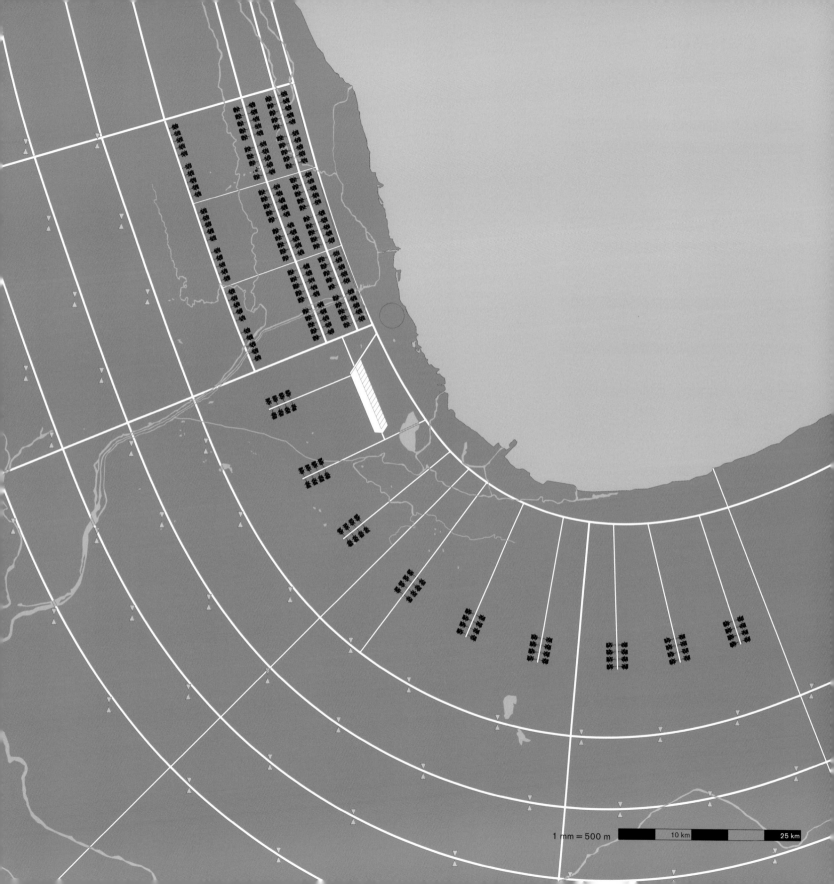

1 mm = 500 m   10 km   25 km

COMMUNITAS 1

USA, 1947
Paul and Percival Goodman

Total Site Area (2-D; in m²)	307,370,996
Total Greenspace (m²)	262,882,979
Area: Greenspace: agriculture	262,882,979
Area: Greenspace: lawn	
Area: Greenspace: park	
Area: Greenspace: wilderness	
Area of Water (m²)	4,719,761
Area of Infrastructure (m²)	44,635,921
Total Built Area [footprint; m²)]	4,190,981
Area: Housing (footprint)	3,014,122
Area: Industrial (footprint)	233,826
Area: Public (footprint)	943,032
Total Population	6,000,000
Total number housing units	
Number of people per housing unit	
Total Area (3-D; in m²)	322,313,934
Number of Floors: Housing	1
Number of Floors: Industrial	6
Number of Floors: Public	6
Area: Total Built	10,075,274
Area: Housing (3-D)	3,014,122
Area: Industrial (3-D)	1,402,958
Area: Public (3-D)	5,658,194
Area: Open Space (Greenspace + Water + Infrastructure) (3-D)	312,238,660
FAR: 3-D Area / 2-D Area (x)	1.05
DENSITY: total population / site area (2-D) (people per km²)	19,520
DENSITY: total population / total area (3-D) (people per km²)	18,615

2-D Percentages	
Greenspace	86%
Agriculture	86%
Lawn	0%
Park	0%
Wilderness	0%
Water	2%
Infrastructure	14%
Built Area	1%
Housing	1%
Industrial	0%
Public	0%
Total % of land use (can exceed 100%)	103%

3-D Percentages	
Greenspace	82%
Agriculture	82%
Lawn	0%
Park	0%
Wilderness	0%
Water	1%
Infrastructure	14%
Built Area	3%
Housing	1%
Industrial	0%
Public	2%
Total % of land use	100%

The best known of the Goodman brothers' multiple Communitas projects, the Community of Efficient Consumption, was an attempt to maximize and streamline functionality and productivity. To this end, the city has a pedestrian, commercial and business center housed in an enormous cylindrical megastructure to encourage all-weather shopping. This center is surrounded by rings of universities and public buildings, and an interconnected network of housing and roadways beyond. Like the other Communitas projects, this community starkly divides the urban setting from nature, and allows direct and easy access across zones to minimize physical and psychological distances.

2D DENSITY RANKING	FAR RANKING	GREENSPACE RANKING	POPULATION RANKING	3D DENSITY RANKING
15/49	42/49	11/49	2/49	9/49

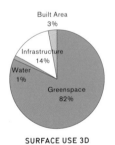

SURFACE USE 3D

Built Area 3%
Infrastructure 14%
Water 1%
Greenspace 82%

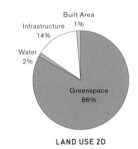

LAND USE 2D

Built Area 1%
Infrastructure 14%
Water 2%
Greenspace 86%

BUILT SPACE

Public 23%
Industrial 6%
Housing 71%

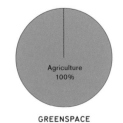

GREENSPACE

Agriculture 100%

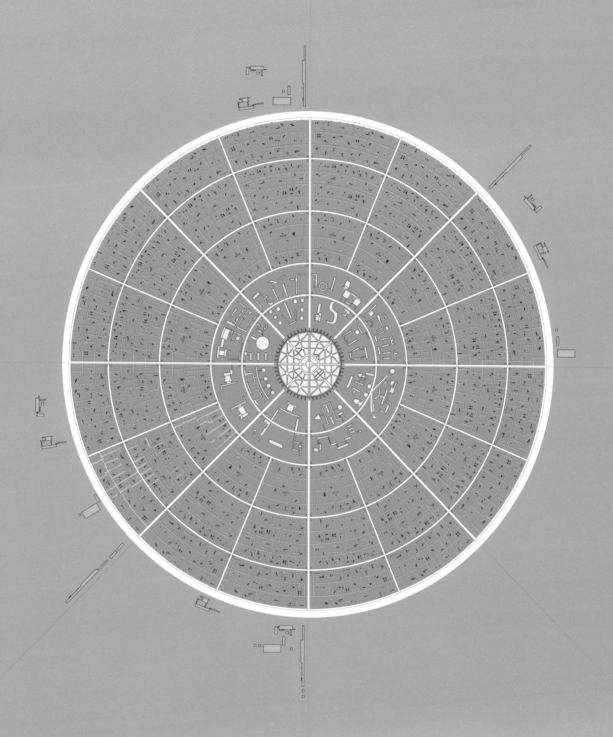

1 mm = 100 m　　　　5 km

Total Site Area (2-D; in m²)	2,721,011,517

Total Greenspace (m²)	2,691,792,887
Area: Greenspace: agriculture	469,166,531
Area: Greenspace: lawn	
Area: Greenspace: park	90,391,463
Area: Greenspace: wilderness	2,132,234,892

Area of Water (m²)	-
Area of Infrastructure (m²)	9,581,063

Total Built Area [footprint; m²)]	14,338,197
Area: Housing (footprint)	8,738,765
Area: Industrial (footprint)	1,156,959
Area: Public (footprint)	4,442,473

Total Population	6,000,000
Total number housing units	
Number of people per housing unit	

Total Area (3-D; in m²)	2,865,795,173
Number of Floors: Housing	6
Number of Floors: Industrial	20
Number of Floors: Public	20
Area: Total Built	164,421,223
Area: Housing (3-D)	52,432,589
Area: Industrial (3-D)	23,139,174
Area: Public (3-D)	88,849,460
Area: Open Space (Greenspace + Water + Infrastructure) (3-D)	2,701,373,950

FAR: 3-D Area / 2-D Area (x)	1.05

DENSITY: total population / site area (2-D) (people per km²)	2,205
DENSITY: total population / total area (3-D) (people per km²)	2,094

2-D Percentages	
Greenspace	99%
Agriculture	18%
Lawn	0%
Park	3%
Wilderness	78%
Water	0%
Infrastructure	0%
Built Area	1%
Housing	1%
Industrial	0%
Public	0%
Total % of land use (can exceed 100%)	100%

3-D Percentages	
Greenspace	94%
Agriculture	17%
Lawn	0%
Park	3%
Wilderness	74%
Water	0%
Infrastructure	0%
Built Area	6%
Housing	2%
Industrial	1%
Public	3%
Total % of land use	100%

The Goodman brothers' series of plans for cities presented in their book *Communitas* propose a libertarian-yet-socialistic urbanism, focused on both efficiency and individual choice. Community with the Elimination of the Difference Between Production and Consumption presents a hexagon-shaped plan with multi-use residential, commercial, public, and industrial sector in the city center, surrounded by a ring of "diversified farms." The scheme strives for a closer relation between personal and productive environments in an attempt to develop a tight local/regional economy. The center of this city is highly dense and irregular—a nod to Camillo Sitte's *City Planning According to Artistic Principles*. The proximity of the urban core to the farms and countryside allows for easy access from one to the other, and the farms are valued for their educational and aesthetic value in addition to their productive use.

2D DENSITY RANKING	FAR RANKING	GREENSPACE RANKING	POPULATION RANKING	3D DENSITY RANKING
41/49	41/49	4/49	1/49★	35/49

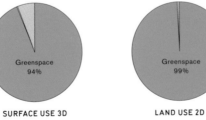

SURFACE USE 3D

LAND USE 2D

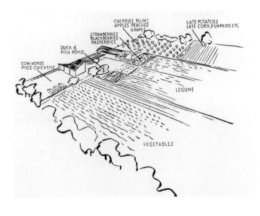

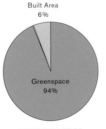

BUILT SPACE

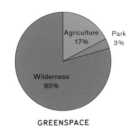

GREENSPACE

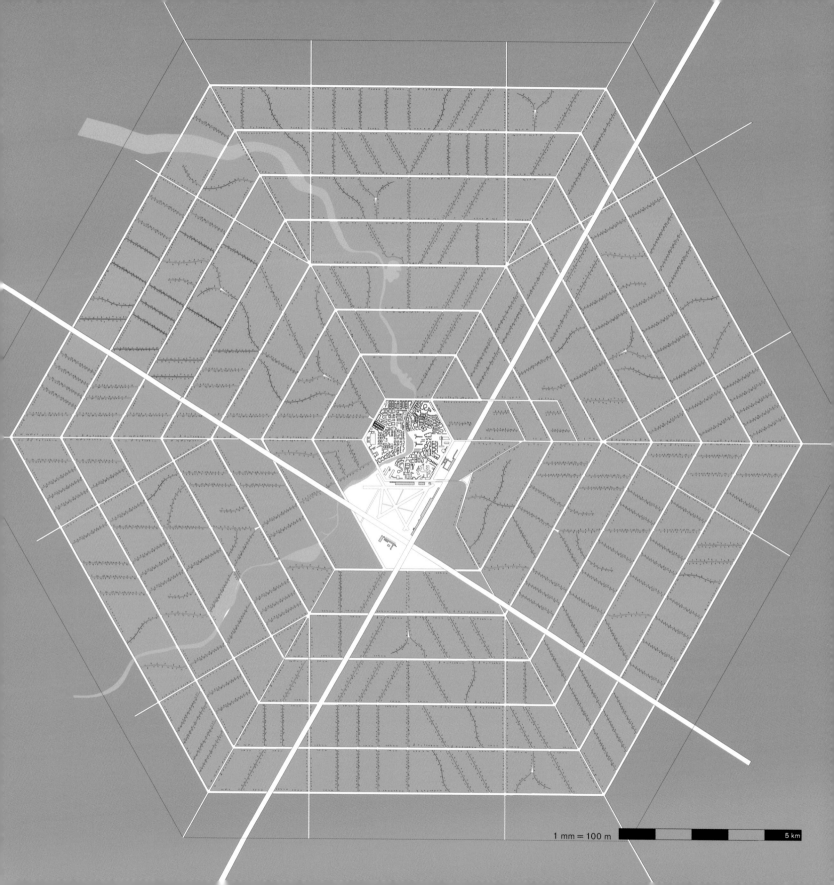

1 mm = 100 m   5 km

Total Site Area (2-D; in m²)	15,360,918

Total Greenspace (m²)	10,605,870
Area: Greenspace: agriculture	0
Area: Greenspace: lawn	7,263,969
Area: Greenspace: park	3,341,901
Area: Greenspace: wilderness	0

Area of Water (m²)	208,740
Area of Infrastructure (m²)	2,143,149

Total Built Area [footprint; m²)]	2,403,159
Area: Housing (footprint)	2,172,034
Area: Industrial (footprint)	141,399
Area: Public (footprint)	89,726

Total Population	70,000
Total number housing units	31,275
Number of people per housing unit	2.24

Total Area (3-D; in m²)	17,532,952
Number of Floors: Housing	2
Number of Floors: Industrial	1
Number of Floors: Public	1
Area: Total Built	4,575,193
Area: Housing (3-D)	4,344,068
Area: Industrial (3-D)	141,399
Area: Public (3-D)	89,726
Area: Open Space (Greenspace + Water + Infrastructure) (3-D)	12,957,759

FAR: 3-D Area / 2-D Area (x)	1.14

DENSITY: total population / site area (2-D) (people per km²)	4,557
DENSITY: total population / total area (3-D) (people per km²)	3,992

2-D Percentages	
Greenspace	69%
Agriculture	0%
Lawn	47%
Park	22%
Wilderness	0%
Water	1%
Infrastructure	14%
Built Area	16%
Housing	14%
Industrial	1%
Public	1%
Total % of land use (can exceed 100%)	100%

3-D Percentages	
Greenspace	60%
Agriculture	0%
Lawn	41%
Park	19%
Wilderness	0%
Water	1%
Infrastructure	13%
Built Area	26%
Housing	24%
Industrial	1%
Public	1%
Total % of land use	100%

Levittown, New York, built from 1947 to 1951 to accommodate returning soldiers starting families, was the first mass-produced suburb. Comprised of six models of houses built on concrete slab foundations, Levittown provided an affordable entry to suburban living for thousands of people wanting to leave New York City. Levittown was divided into master blocks of roughly one square mile, which were in turn subdivided into "sections," each containing 300 to 500 houses. Each neighborhood had a public school, and main thoroughfares featured churches, public facilities, and shopping. Residential streets were designed as "traffic-calming": curvilinear and without four-way intersections; a number of greenbelts were interspersed throughout the neighborhoods. While initially derided as extremely homogenous, the residents of Levittown have modified and added on to their homes so extensively that few unaltered houses remain.

2D DENSITY RANKING	FAR RANKING	GREENSPACE RANKING	POPULATION RANKING	3D DENSITY RANKING
28/49	37/49	19/49	21/49	22/49

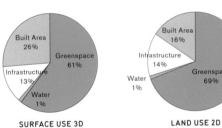

SURFACE USE 3D   LAND USE 2D

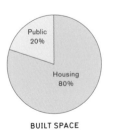 

BUILT SPACE   GREENSPACE

1 mm = 40 m ▮▮▮▮ 1 km ▮▮▮▮ 2 km

1 mm = 10 m ▮▮▮▮▮▮▮▮ 500 m

FORT WORTH

Texas, USA, 1956
Victor Gruen

Total Site Area (2-D; in m²)	**1,467,137**
Total Greenspace (m²)	**465,467**
Area: Greenspace: agriculture	0
Area: Greenspace: lawn	0
Area: Greenspace: park	465,467
Area: Greenspace: wilderness	0
Area of Water (m²)	**0**
Area of Infrastructure (m²)	**274,070**
Total Built Area [footprint; m²)]	**727,600**
Area: Housing (footprint)	0
Area: Industrial (footprint)	0
Area: Public (footprint)	727,600
Total Population	**100,000**
Total number housing units	n/a
Number of people per housing unit	n/a
Total Area (3-D; in m²)	**7,287,938**
Number of Floors: Housing	0
Number of Floors: Industrial	0
Number of Floors: Public	9
Area: Total Built	**6,548,401**
Area: Housing (3-D)	0
Area: Industrial (3-D)	0
Area: Public (3-D)	6,548,401
Area: Open Space (Greenspace + Water + Infrastructure) (3-D)	739,537
FAR: 3-D Area / 2-D Area (x)	**4.97**
DENSITY: total population / site area (2-D) (people per km²)	**68,160**
DENSITY: total population / total area (3-D) (people per km²)	**13,721**

2-D Percentages		
Greenspace		**32%**
Agriculture	0%	
Lawn	0%	
Park	32%	
Wilderness	0%	
Water		**0%**
Infrastructure		**18%**
Built Area		**50%**
Housing	0%	
Industrial	0%	
Public	50%	
Total % of land use (can exceed 100%)		**100%**

3-D Percentages		
Greenspace		**6%**
Agriculture	0%	
Lawn	0%	
Park	6%	
Wilderness	0%	
Water		**0%**
Infrastructure		**4%**
Built Area		**90%**
Housing	0%	
Industrial	0%	
Public	90%	
Total % of land use		**100%**

Victor Gruen, an Austrian-born urban planner known mainly for essentially inventing the suburban shopping mall, went on to later propose car-free pedestrian city centers around the US, including a major revitalization plan for Fort Worth. His project for a European-style pedestrian network in downtown Fort Worth featured "businesses-on-a-podium" with garages interspersed throughout, easily accessible from a new ring road. In the creation of this dense core, Gruen wanted to interrupt the "sterile, grid-iron street pattern" with plazas and land-scaped squares, in order to make streets "more surprising, more compact, more variegated, and busier," according to Jane Jacobs.

2D DENSITY RANKING	FAR RANKING	GREENSPACE RANKING	POPULATION RANKING	3D DENSITY RANKING
7/49	**7/49**	**31/49**	**19/49**	**12/49**

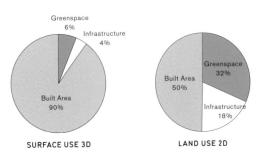

SURFACE USE 3D — Built Area 90%, Greenspace 6%, Infrastructure 4%

LAND USE 2D — Built Area 50%, Greenspace 32%, Infrastructure 18%

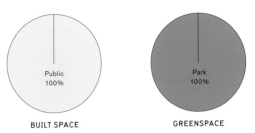

BUILT SPACE — Public 100%

GREENSPACE — Park 100%

1 mm = 10 m   500 m

 # BRASILIA

Brazil, 1957
Lucio Costa

Total Site Area (2-D; in m²)	**69,037,902**
Total Greenspace (m²)	**57,064,934**
Area: Greenspace: agriculture	
Area: Greenspace: lawn	
Area: Greenspace: park	14,149,328
Area: Greenspace: wilderness	42,915,606
Area of Water (m²)	**-**
Area of Infrastructure (m²)	**9,918,503**
Total Built Area [footprint; m²)]	**2,054,465**
Area: Housing (footprint)	1,134,097
Area: Industrial (footprint)	181,238
Area: Public (footprint)	739,131
Total Population	**140,000**
Total number housing units	
Number of people per housing unit	
Total Area (3-D; in m²)	**82,331,731**
Number of Floors: Housing	8
Number of Floors: Industrial	2
Number of Floors: Public	8
Area: Total Built	**15,348,294**
Area: Housing (3-D)	9,072,773
Area: Industrial (3-D)	362,476
Area: Public (3-D)	5,913,046
Area: Open Space (Greenspace + Water + Infrastructure) (3-D)	66,983,437
FAR: 3-D Area / 2-D Area (x)	**1.19**
DENSITY: total population / site area (2-D) (people per km²)	**2,028**
DENSITY: total population / total area (3-D) (people per km²)	**1,700**

2-D Percentages	
Greenspace	**83%**
Agriculture	0%
Lawn	0%
Park	21%
Wilderness	62%
Water	**0%**
Infrastructure	**14%**
Built Area	**3%**
Housing	2%
Industrial	0%
Public	1%
Total % of land use (can exceed 100%)	**100%**

3-D Percentages	
Greenspace	**69%**
Agriculture	0%
Lawn	0%
Park	17%
Wilderness	52%
Water	**0%**
Infrastructure	**12%**
Built Area	**19%**
Housing	12%
Industrial	0%
Public	7%
Total % of land use	**100%**

Lucio Costa and Oscar Niemeyer's Brasilia was constructed from 1956 to 1960 as Brazil's new capital city, in an attempt to rectify regional inequalities. Closely following the principles of CIAM's Athens Charter, the Radiant City-inspired plan was superimposed on the jungle landscape in the shape of a open-winged bird. The north-south monumental administrative axis at the center of the city was flanked on either side by residential blocks. These subdivisions, known as *superquadras*, uniformly contained several Modernist mid-rise apartment building slabs, local commercial enterprises like cinemas and shops and public amenities like schools.

2D DENSITY RANKING	FAR RANKING	GREENSPACE RANKING	POPULATION RANKING	3D DENSITY RANKING
43/49	**33/49**	**12/49**	**17/49**	**37/49**

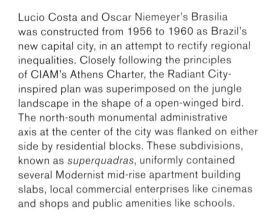

SURFACE USE 3D — Built Area 19%, Greenspace 69%, Infrastructure 12%

LAND USE 2D — Built Area 3%, Infrastructure 14%, Greenspace 83%

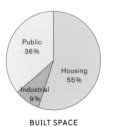

BUILT SPACE — Public 36%, Housing 55%, Industrial 9%

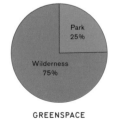

GREENSPACE — Park 25%, Wilderness 75%

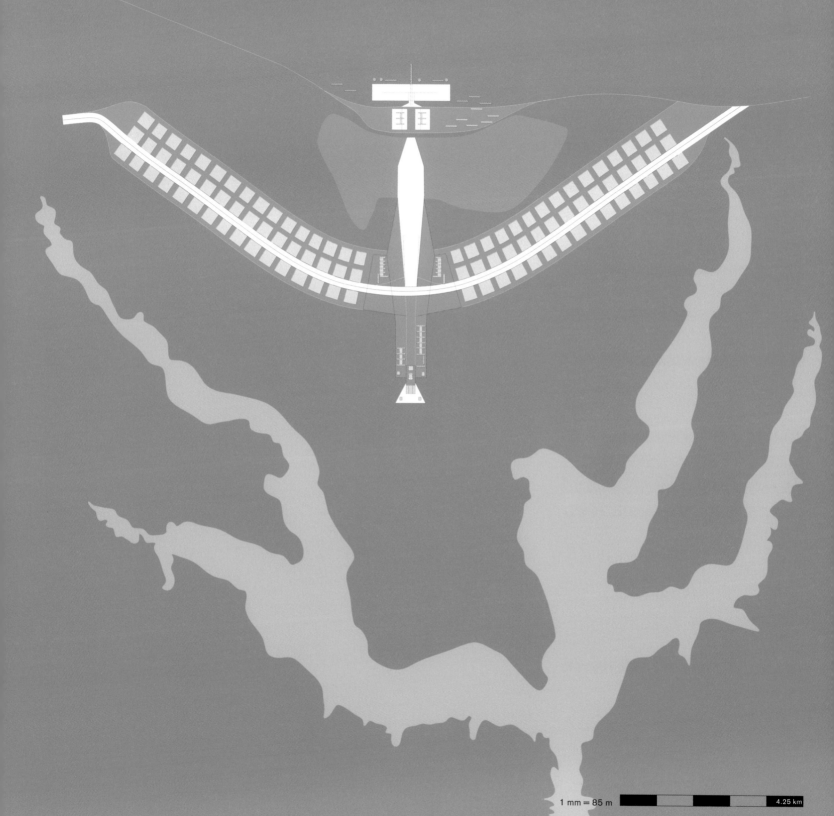

1 mm = 85 m   4.25 km

Berlin, Germany, 1958
Alison and Peter Smithson

Total Site Area (2-D; in m²)	**6,924,114**
Total Greenspace (m²)	**4,164,865**
Area: Greenspace: agriculture	-
Area: Greenspace: lawn	1,536,460
Area: Greenspace: park	2,628,405
Area: Greenspace: wilderness	-
Area of Water (m²)	**102,871**
Area of Infrastructure (m²)	**2,064,413**
Total Built Area [footprint; m²)]	**591,965**
Area: Housing (footprint)	135,814
Area: Industrial (footprint)	-
Area: Public (footprint)	456,151
Total Population	**100,000**
Total number housing units	n/a
Number of people per housing unit	n/a
Total Area (3-D; in m²)	**9,883,938**
Number of Floors: Housing	6
Number of Floors: Industrial	-
Number of Floors: Public	6
Area: Total Built	**3,551,790**
Area: Housing (3-D)	814,883
Area: Industrial (3-D)	-
Area: Public (3-D)	2,736,906
Area: Open Space (Greenspace + Water + Infrastructure) (3-D)	6,332,149
FAR: 3-D Area / 2-D Area (x)	**1.43**
DENSITY: total population / site area (2-D) (people per km²)	**14,442**
DENSITY: total population / total area (3-D) (people per km²)	**10,117**

2-D Percentages	
Greenspace	**60%**
Agriculture	0%
Lawn	22%
Park	38%
Wilderness	0%
Water	**1%**
Infrastructure	**30%**
Built Area	**9%**
Housing	2%
Industrial	0%
Public	7%
Total % of land use (can exceed 100%)	**100%**

3-D Percentages	
Greenspace	**42%**
Agriculture	0%
Lawn	16%
Park	26%
Wilderness	0%
Water	**1%**
Infrastructure	**21%**
Built Area	**36%**
Housing	8%
Industrial	0%
Public	28%
Total % of land use	**100%**

The Hauptstadt plan was the Smithsons' entry for a competition to rebuild the central business district of Berlin. The proposal was for a megastructural mat-building incorporating both existing historical structures and new office towers. It was to be constructed above the existing street grid, designed to house multiple levels of circulation with a pedestrian deck on top and transport below. As an early example of Team 10's approach, the Smithsons' design was driven by a reaction to the rigid geometries and orthodoxy of CIAM, attempting to create an "organic and playful" urban environment.

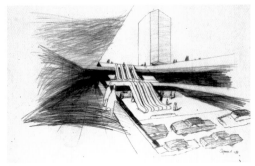

2D DENSITY RANKING	FAR RANKING	GREENSPACE RANKING	POPULATION RANKING	3D DENSITY RANKING
18/49	29/49	25/49	18/49	13/49

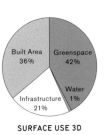

SURFACE USE 3D

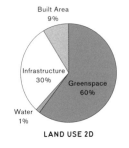

LAND USE 2D

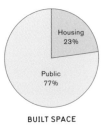

BUILT SPACE

GREENSPACE

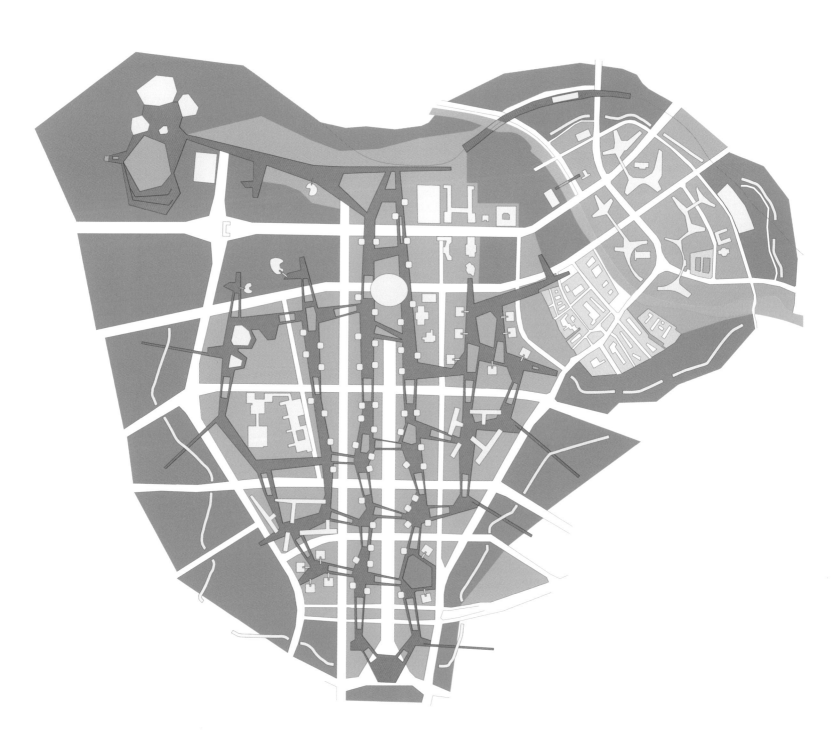

1 mm = 35 m   875 m   1750 m

AGRICULTURAL CITY

Rural Japan, 1960
Kisho Kurokawa

Total Site Area (2-D; in m²)	**1,151,836**
Total Greenspace (m²)	**1,088,070**
Area: Greenspace: agriculture	1,088,070
Area: Greenspace: lawn	0
Area: Greenspace: park	0
Area: Greenspace: wilderness	0
Area of Water (m²)	**0**
Area of Infrastructure (m²)	**0**
Total Built Area [footprint; m²)]	**63,766**
Area: Housing (footprint)	24,607
Area: Industrial (footprint)	0
Area: Public (footprint)	39,159
Total Population	**5,000**
Total number housing units	
Number of people per housing unit	
Total Area (3-D; in m²)	**1,279,367**
Number of Floors: Housing	3
Number of Floors: Industrial	0
Number of Floors: Public	3
Area: Total Built	**191,297**
Area: Housing (3-D)	73,821
Area: Industrial (3-D)	0
Area: Public (3-D)	117,476
Area: Open Space (Greenspace + Water + Infrastructure) (3-D)	1,088,070
FAR: 3-D Area / 2-D Area (x)	**1.11**
DENSITY: total population / site area (2-D) (people per km²)	**4,341**
DENSITY: total population / total area (3-D) (people per km²)	**3,908**

2-D Percentages		
Greenspace		**94%**
Agriculture	94%	
Lawn	0%	
Park	0%	
Wilderness	0%	
Water		**0%**
Infrastructure		**0%**
Built Area		**6%**
Housing	2%	
Industrial	0%	
Public	4%	
Total % of land use (can exceed 100%)		**100%**

3-D Percentages		
Greenspace		**85%**
Agriculture	85%	
Lawn	0%	
Park	0%	
Wilderness	0%	
Water		**0%**
Infrastructure		**0%**
Built Area		**15%**
Housing	6%	
Industrial	0%	
Public	9%	
Total % of land use		**100%**

The Agricultural City, Kisho Kurokawa's project for a contemporaization of Japanese farm villages, incorporates the Metabolists' high-density ideal within a rural setting. Kurokawa's gridiron network of raised platforms attempts to achieve uniform and maximum organization of farm life, including residential areas and markets, as well as the infrastructure required to organize farm products for delivery to surrounding cities. The project includes pedestrian decks above grade and networks for information and energy distribution. These networks link housing and other buildings, which are essentially individual, autonomous structures that Kurokawa imagined to be individually designed and developed by the villagers within certain loose planning guidelines.

2D DENSITY RANKING	FAR RANKING	GREENSPACE RANKING	POPULATION RANKING	3D DENSITY RANKING
30/49	38/49	7/49	39/49	24/49

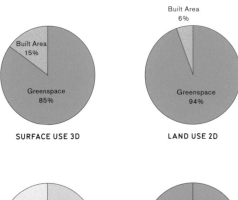

SURFACE USE 3D

LAND USE 2D

BUILT SPACE

GREENSPACE

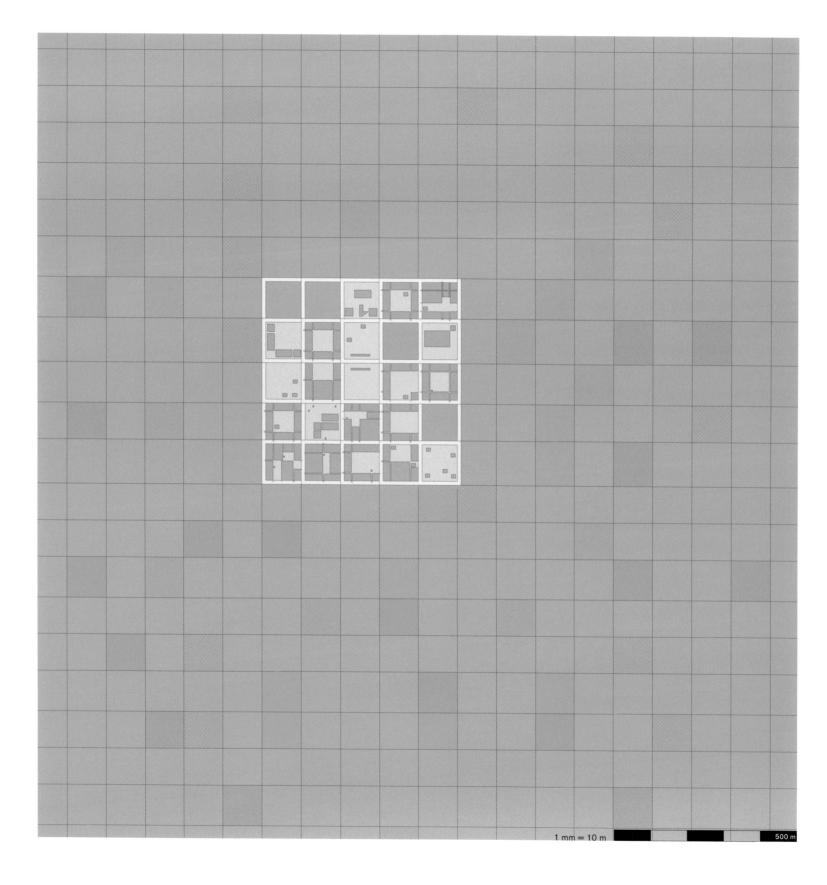

1 mm = 10 m   500 m

DOME OVER MANHATTAN

Total Site Area (2-D; in m²)	**8,133,210**
Total Greenspace (m²)	**731,989**
Area: Greenspace: agriculture	0
Area: Greenspace: lawn	121,998
Area: Greenspace: park	609,991
Area: Greenspace: wilderness	0
Area of Water (m²)	**5,074**
Area of Infrastructure (m²)	**2,927,956**
Total Built Area [footprint; m²)]	**4,473,266**
Area: Housing (footprint)	1,789,306
Area: Industrial (footprint)	2,326,098
Area: Public (footprint)	357,861
Total Population	**800,000**
Total number housing units	320,000
Number of people per housing unit	2.5
Total Area (3-D; in m²)	**22,289,907**
Number of Floors: Housing	5
Number of Floors: Industrial	4
Number of Floors: Public	2
Area: Total Built	**18,624,888**
Area: Housing (3-D)	9,744,562
Area: Industrial (3-D)	8,164,604
Area: Public (3-D)	715,722
Area: Open Space (Greenspace + Water + Infrastructure) (3-D)	3,665,019
FAR: 3-D Area / 2-D Area (x)	**2.74**
DENSITY: total population / site area (2-D) (people per km²)	**98,362**
DENSITY: total population / total area (3-D) (people per km²)	**35,891**

2-D Percentages		
Greenspace		**9%**
Agriculture	0%	
Lawn	2%	
Park	8%	
Wilderness	0%	
Water		**0%**
Infrastructure		**36%**
Built Area		**55%**
Housing	22%	
Industrial	29%	
Public	4%	
Total % of land use (can exceed 100%)		**100%**

3-D Percentages		
Greenspace		**3%**
Agriculture	0%	
Lawn	1%	
Park	2%	
Wilderness	0%	
Water		**0%**
Infrastructure		**13%**
Built Area		**84%**
Housing	44%	
Industrial	37%	
Public	3%	
Total % of land use		**100%**

One of Buckminster Fuller's numerous domed projects, the Dome over Manhattan was an attempt to rectify the wasteful nature of the urban environment. The dome would keep warmth inside, and prevent rain and snow from entering the business core of the city. Fuller was obsessed with the efficiency of a climate-free city, citing the enormous savings in elements such as snow removal to promote its superiority over traditional urban development.

2D DENSITY RANKING	FAR RANKING	GREENSPACE RANKING	POPULATION RANKING	3D DENSITY RANKING
4/49	**14/49**	**42/49**	**8/49**	**2/49**

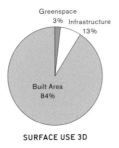

SURFACE USE 3D

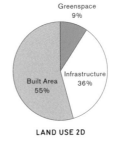

LAND USE 2D

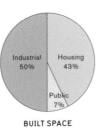

BUILT SPACE

GREENSPACE

1 mm = 50 m   1250 m   2500 m

MESA CITY

Total Site Area (2-D; in m²)	788,311,717

Total Greenspace (m²)	692,255,048
Area: Greenspace: agriculture	0
Area: Greenspace: lawn	0
Area: Greenspace: park	62,218,596
Area: Greenspace: wilderness	630,036,452

Area of Water (m²)	31,808,788
Area of Infrastructure (m²)	38,659,280

Total Built Area [footprint; m²)]	25,588,600
Area: Housing (footprint)	9,313,106
Area: Industrial (footprint)	0
Area: Public (footprint)	16,275,495

Total Population	2,000,000
Total number housing units	
Number of people per housing unit	

Total Area (3-D; in m²)	4,204,084,187
Number of Floors: Housing	20
Number of Floors: Industrial	
Number of Floors: Public	200
Area: Total Built	3,441,361,070
Area: Housing (3-D)	186,262,110
Area: Industrial (3-D)	-
Area: Public (3-D)	3,255,098,960
Area: Open Space (Greenspace + Water + Infrastructure) (3-D)	762,723,116

FAR: 3-D Area / 2-D Area (x)	5.33

DENSITY: total population / site area (2-D) (people per km²)	2,537
DENSITY: total population / total area (3-D) (people per km²)	476

2-D Percentages	
Greenspace	88%
Agriculture	0%
Lawn	0%
Park	8%
Wilderness	80%
Water	4%
Infrastructure	5%
Built Area	3%
Housing	1%
Industrial	0%
Public	2%
Total % of land use (can exceed 100%)	100%

3-D Percentages	
Greenspace	16%
Agriculture	0%
Lawn	0%
Park	1%
Wilderness	15%
Water	1%
Infrastructure	1%
Built Area	82%
Housing	5%
Industrial	0%
Public	77%
Total % of land use	100%

Mesa City, an early urban project by Paolo Soleri, proposed situating a series of megastructural compounds on an arid highland. The city, about the size of Manhattan, features a residential and academic complex at its north end, and administrative and public functions to the south, with multiple buildings throughout the site reaching 1,000 meters high. The city is ringed by a road network that houses commercial enterprises and industry. A canyon-park runs up the center of the scheme, flanked by agricultural areas that are irrigated by canals. The self-contained city generates its own energy from solar, hydro, and wind power, and the compact footprint of built structures leaves a large amount of open space around it.

2D DENSITY RANKING	FAR RANKING	GREENSPACE RANKING	POPULATION RANKING	3D DENSITY RANKING
37/49	5/49	9/49	6/49	48/49

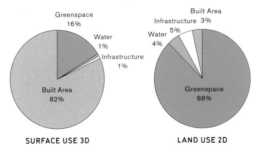

SURFACE USE 3D   LAND USE 2D

BUILT SPACE   GREENSPACE

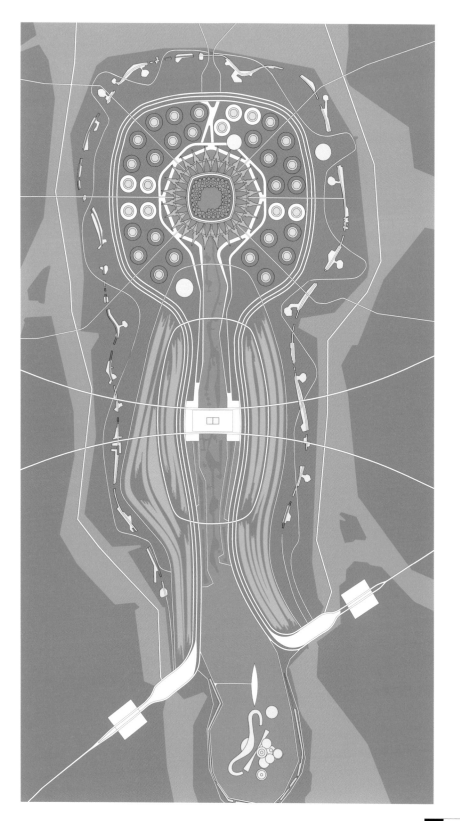

1 mm = 200 m ████░░░░████ 5 km ████░░░░████ 10km

Total Site Area (2-D; in m²)	**13,722,107**

Total Greenspace (m²)	**-**
Area: Greenspace: agriculture	-
Area: Greenspace: lawn	-
Area: Greenspace: park	-
Area: Greenspace: wilderness	-

Area of Water (m²)	**-**
Area of Infrastructure (m²)	**13,016,486**

Total Built Area [footprint; m²)]	**705,621**
Area: Housing (footprint)	-
Area: Industrial (footprint)	-
Area: Public (footprint)	705,621

Total Population	**500,000**
Total number housing units	n/a
Number of people per housing unit	n/a

Total Area (3-D; in m²)	**15,838,970**
Number of Floors: Housing	4
Number of Floors: Industrial	4
Number of Floors: Public	4
Area: Total Built	**2,822,484**
Area: Housing (3-D)	-
Area: Industrial (3-D)	-
Area: Public (3-D)	2,822,484
Area: Open Space (Greenspace + Water + Infrastructure) (3-D)	13,016,486

FAR: 3-D Area / 2-D Area (x)	**1.15**

DENSITY: total population / site area (2-D) (people per km²)	**36,438**
DENSITY: total population / total area (3-D) (people per km²)	**31,568**

2-D Percentages	
Greenspace	**0%**
Agriculture	0%
Lawn	0%
Park	0%
Wilderness	0%
Water	**0%**
Infrastructure	**95%**
Built Area	**5%**
Housing	0%
Industrial	0%
Public	5%
Total % of land use (can exceed 100%)	**100%**

3-D Percentages	
Greenspace	**0%**
Agriculture	0%
Lawn	0%
Park	0%
Wilderness	0%
Water	**0%**
Infrastructure	**82%**
Built Area	**18%**
Housing	0%
Industrial	0%
Public	18%
Total % of land use	**100%**

Constant's project for a Situationist city, New Babylon, was essentially an infinite mega-structure spanning the entirety of the Earth's surface. Its occupants, homo ludens ("man the player"), would participate in a constant psychogeographic "drift" through its sectors, comprised of space-frames hanging off support towers. The interior of each sector would be an indeterminate arrangement of large and small spaces, whose position was to be decided on by occupants. These flexible, unprogrammed sectors would then link together, surrounding, but not infiltrating, existing city centers.

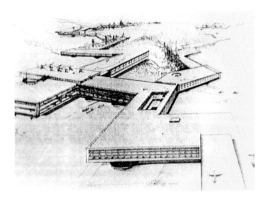

2D DENSITY RANKING	FAR RANKING	GREENSPACE RANKING	POPULATION RANKING	3D DENSITY RANKING
9/49	35/49	46/49	12/49	4/49

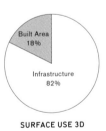

SURFACE USE 3D

Built Area 18%
Infrastructure 82%

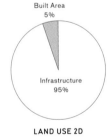

LAND USE 2D

Built Area 5%
Infrastructure 95%

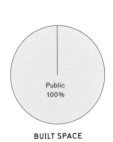

BUILT SPACE

Public 100%

1 mm = 35 m   875 m   1750 m

 # OCEAN CITY

Unabara, Japan, 1960
Kiyonori Kitutake

Total Site Area (2-D; in m²)	**198,849,635**
Total Greenspace (m²)	**609,775**
Area: Greenspace: agriculture	0
Area: Greenspace: lawn	0
Area: Greenspace: park	609,775
Area: Greenspace: wilderness	0
Area of Water (m²)	**88,525,632**
Area of Infrastructure (m²)	**107,179,167**
Total Built Area [footprint; m²)]	**2,535,061**
Area: Housing (footprint)	354,540
Area: Industrial (footprint)	408,407
Area: Public (footprint)	1,772,114
Total Population	**500,000**
Total number housing units	360,000
Number of people per housing unit	1.39
Total Area (3-D; in m²)	**219,736,906**
Number of Floors: Housing	54
Number of Floors: Industrial	2
Number of Floors: Public	2
Area: Total Built	**23,422,332**
Area: Housing (3-D)	19,061,290
Area: Industrial (3-D)	816,814
Area: Public (3-D)	3,544,227
Area: Open Space (Greenspace + Water + Infrastructure) (3-D)	196,314,574
FAR: 3-D Area / 2-D Area (x)	**1.11**
DENSITY: total population / site area (2-D) (people per km²)	**2,514**
DENSITY: total population / total area (3-D) (people per km²)	**2,275**

2-D Percentages	
Greenspace	**0%**
Agriculture	0%
Lawn	0%
Park	0%
Wilderness	0%
Water	**45%**
Infrastructure	**54%**
Built Area	**1%**
Housing	0%
Industrial	0%
Public	1%
Total % of land use (can exceed 100%)	**100%**

3-D Percentages	
Greenspace	**0%**
Agriculture	0%
Lawn	0%
Park	0%
Wilderness	0%
Water	**40%**
Infrastructure	**49%**
Built Area	**11%**
Housing	9%
Industrial	0%
Public	2%
Total % of land use	**100%**

Kiyonori Kikutake's Ocean City was a Metabolist proposal for a floating city of two concentric rings. The inner ring is reserved for residential uses, the outer is designated as an industrial zone, and the innermost islands are to be used for communal purposes. The area between the rings is reserved for the cultivation and production of special sea products, while the meeting point of the rings provides a space for a communal administration and planning center. The city is governed by a "control tower," which provides artificial sunlight to the whole city; new towers are set up as the city expands with each tower acting as a nucleus. "Mova-blocks" compose the housing in the Ocean City, with each housing unit as an exchangeable circular house that can revolve around the core. At 100 meters high, each tower houses 10,000 people.

2D DENSITY RANKING	FAR RANKING	GREENSPACE RANKING	POPULATION RANKING	3D DENSITY RANKING
38/49	**40/49**	**44/49**	**11/49**	**31/49**

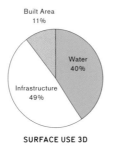

SURFACE USE 3D

Built Area 11%
Water 40%
Infrastructure 49%

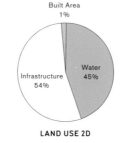

LAND USE 2D

Built Area 1%
Water 45%
Infrastructure 54%

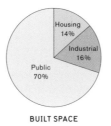

BUILT SPACE

Housing 14%
Industrial 16%
Public 70%

GREENSPACE

Park 100%

1 mm = 100 m   5 km

Tokyo, Japan, 1960
Kenzo Tange

Total Site Area (2-D; in m²)	**1,047,313,950**
Total Greenspace (m²)	**31,341,294**
Area: Greenspace: agriculture	0
Area: Greenspace: lawn	0
Area: Greenspace: park	31,341,294
Area: Greenspace: wilderness	0
Area of Water (m²)	**764,456,587**
Area of Infrastructure (m²)	**47,123,465**
Total Built Area [footprint; m²)]	**204,392,604**
Area: Housing (footprint)	52,738,456
Area: Industrial (footprint)	149,018,069
Area: Public (footprint)	2,636,079
Total Population	**5,000,000**
Total number housing units	
Number of people per housing unit	
Total Area (3-D; in m²)	**1,467,932,538**
Number of Floors: Housing	6
Number of Floors: Industrial	2
Number of Floors: Public	4
Area: Total Built	**625,011,192**
Area: Housing (3-D)	316,430,739
Area: Industrial (3-D)	298,036,138
Area: Public (3-D)	10,544,315
Area: Open Space (Greenspace + Water + Infrastructure) (3-D)	842,921,346
FAR: 3-D Area / 2-D Area (x)	**1.40**
DENSITY: total population / site area (2-D) (people per km²)	**4,774**
DENSITY: total population / total area (3-D) (people per km²)	**3,406**

2-D Percentages	
Greenspace	**3%**
Agriculture	0%
Lawn	0%
Park	3%
Wilderness	0%
Water	**73%**
Infrastructure	**4%**
Built Area	**20%**
Housing	6%
Industrial	14%
Public	0%
Total % of land use (can exceed 100%)	**100%**

3-D Percentages	
Greenspace	**2%**
Agriculture	0%
Lawn	0%
Park	2%
Wilderness	0%
Water	**52%**
Infrastructure	**3%**
Built Area	**43%**
Housing	22%
Industrial	20%
Public	1%
Total % of land use	**100%**

Kenzo Tange's massively scaled plan for expanding Tokyo along Metabolist principles centered on creating an enormous central, infrastructural spine jutting into Tokyo Bay. This spine would contain a civic axis of governmental and business districts and would grow the city in a line out from the existing urban agglomeration. The spine would be flanked by high-speed roads without intersections, and the islands themselves would feature buildings on pilotis, to allow the ground plane to be used communally. Housing branches would extend at 90-degree angles from the central spine, and be connected to the core by a monorail system. Industrial areas would be created on landfill near the existing shoreline. Like most other Metabolist projects, the Tokyo Bay expansion could accommodate the addition of both individual units and large sectors in a "tree"-like manner.

2D DENSITY RANKING	FAR RANKING	GREENSPACE RANKING	POPULATION RANKING	3D DENSITY RANKING
27/49	30/49	43/49	3/49	27/49

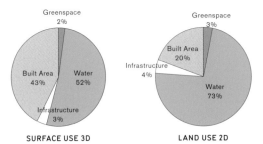

SURFACE USE 3D — Greenspace 2%, Built Area 43%, Water 52%, Infrastructure 3%

LAND USE 2D — Greenspace 3%, Built Area 20%, Infrastructure 4%, Water 73%

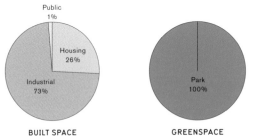

BUILT SPACE — Public 1%, Housing 26%, Industrial 73%

GREENSPACE — Park 100%

1 mm = 100 m   5 km

HELIX CITY

Tokyo, Japan, 1961
Kisho Kurokawa

Total Site Area (2-D; in m²)	**49,068,419**

Total Greenspace (m²)	**7,914,552**
Area: Greenspace: agriculture	0
Area: Greenspace: lawn	0
Area: Greenspace: park	0
Area: Greenspace: wilderness	7,914,552

Area of Water (m²)	**20,759,381**
Area of Infrastructure (m²)	**3,017,093**

Total Built Area [footprint; m²)]	**17,377,393**
Area: Housing (footprint)	15,895,036
Area: Industrial (footprint)	0
Area: Public (footprint)	1,482,358

Total Population	**480,000**
Total number housing units	120,000
Number of people per housing unit	4.00

Total Area (3-D; in m²)	**673,421,878**
Number of Floors: Housing	40
Number of Floors: Industrial	0
Number of Floors: Public	4
Area: Total Built	**641,730,852**
Area: Housing (3-D)	635,801,421
Area: Industrial (3-D)	0
Area: Public (3-D)	5,929,431
Area: Open Space (Greenspace + Water + Infrastructure) (3-D)	31,691,026

FAR: 3-D Area / 2-D Area (x)	**13.72**

DENSITY: total population / site area (2-D) (people per km²)	**9,782**
DENSITY: total population / total area (3-D) (people per km²)	**713**

2-D Percentages	
Greenspace	**17%**
Agriculture	0%
Lawn	0%
Park	0%
Wilderness	16%
Water	**42%**
Infrastructure	**6%**
Built Area	**35%**
Housing	32%
Industrial	0%
Public	3%
Total % of land use (can exceed 100%)	**100%**

3-D Percentages	
Greenspace	**2%**
Agriculture	0%
Lawn	0%
Park	1%
Wilderness	1%
Water	**3%**
Infrastructure	**0%**
Built Area	**95%**
Housing	94%
Industrial	0%
Public	1%
Total % of land use	**100%**

Kisho Kurokawa's Helix City was one of a number of Metabolist urban visions that was to grow from an existing city outward on the surface of a body of water. The helical megastructures comprising the city allow for a plug-in style occupation of their levels; the city expands both by adding units within each helix and by adding new towers. The levels of the helixes were proposed to be completely covered in gardens, allowing for a maximal green surface.

2D DENSITY RANKING	FAR RANKING	GREENSPACE RANKING	POPULATION RANKING	3D DENSITY RANKING
20/49	2/49	38/49	13/49	45/49

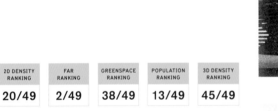

SURFACE USE 3D

LAND USE 2D

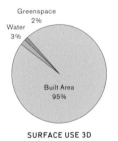

BUILT SPACE

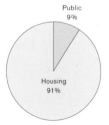

GREENSPACE

Helix City Plan for Tokyo | Japan 1961

1 mm = 100 m   5 km

Total Site Area (2-D; in m²)	429,945

Total Greenspace (m²)	0
Area: Greenspace: agriculture	0
Area: Greenspace: lawn	0
Area: Greenspace: park	0
Area: Greenspace: wilderness	0

Area of Water (m²)	0
Area of Infrastructure (m²)	357,506

Total Built Area [footprint; m²)]	72,439
Area: Housing (footprint)	44,787
Area: Industrial (footprint)	0
Area: Public (footprint)	27,652

Total Population	1,792
Total number housing units	896
Number of people per housing unit	2.00

Total Area (3-D; in m²)	740,733
Number of Floors: Housing	3
Number of Floors: Industrial	0
Number of Floors: Public	9
Area: Total Built	383,227
Area: Housing (3-D)	134,362
Area: Industrial (3-D)	0
Area: Public (3-D)	248,865
Area: Open Space (Greenspace + Water + Infrastructure) (3-D)	357,506

FAR: 3-D Area / 2-D Area (x)	1.72

DENSITY: total population / site area (2-D) (people per km²)	4,168
DENSITY: total population / total area (3-D) (people per km²)	2,419

2-D Percentages		
Greenspace		0%
Agriculture	0%	
Lawn	0%	
Park	0%	
Wilderness	0%	
Water		0%
Infrastructure		83%
Built Area		17%
Housing	11%	
Industrial	0%	
Public	6%	
Total % of land use (can exceed 100%)		100%

3-D Percentages		
Greenspace		0%
Agriculture	0%	
Lawn	0%	
Park	0%	
Wilderness	0%	
Water		0%
Infrastructure		48%
Built Area		52%
Housing	18%	
Industrial	0%	
Public	34%	
Total % of land use		100%

Arata Isozaki's Clusters in the Air proposed a series of vertical cores that would accommodate residences. The vertical core "trees" (a favorite analogy of the Metabolists) provide paths for public transport, while the "branches" serve as lateral paths of movement from the cores. Finally the "leaves," or residential capsules, would connect to the branches. These cluster trees would then multiply above the existing city to create a "forest."

2D DENSITY RANKING	FAR RANKING	GREENSPACE RANKING	POPULATION RANKING	3D DENSITY RANKING
32/49	21/49	49/49	45/49	30/49

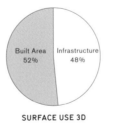

SURFACE USE 3D

Built Area 52% / Infrastructure 48%

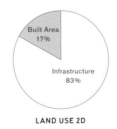

LAND USE 2D

Built Area 17% / Infrastructure 83%

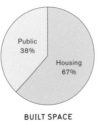

BUILT SPACE

Public 38% / Housing 67%

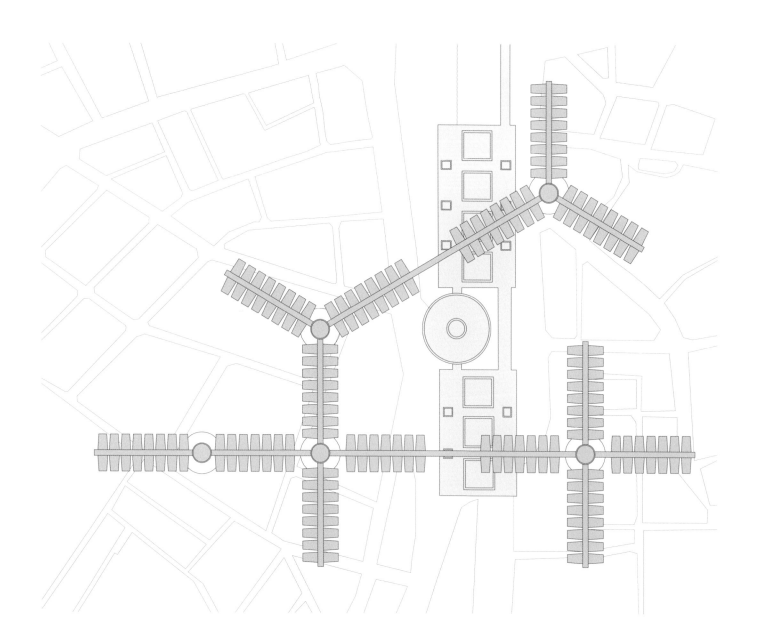

1 mm = 4 m   100 m   200 m

LE MIRAIL

Toulouse, France, 1962
Candilis-Josic-Woods

Total Site Area (2-D; in m²)	**3,054,264**
Total Greenspace (m²)	**1,888,463**
Area: Greenspace: agriculture	-
Area: Greenspace: lawn	-
Area: Greenspace: park	1,888,463
Area: Greenspace: wilderness	-
Area of Water (m²)	**34,499**
Area of Infrastructure (m²)	**697,979**
Total Built Area [footprint; m²)]	**433,323**
Area: Housing (footprint)	172,357
Area: Industrial (footprint)	9,264
Area: Public (footprint)	251,703
Total Population	**45,000**
Total number housing units	?
Number of people per housing unit	?
Total Area (3-D; in m²)	**5,211,155**
Number of Floors: Housing	12
Number of Floors: Industrial	2
Number of Floors: Public	2
Area: Total Built	**2,590,214**
Area: Housing (3-D)	2,068,281
Area: Industrial (3-D)	18,527
Area: Public (3-D)	503,405
Area: Open Space (Greenspace + Water + Infrastructure) (3-D)	2,620,941
FAR: 3-D Area / 2-D Area (x)	**1.71**
DENSITY: total population / site area (2-D) (people per km²)	**14,733**
DENSITY: total population / total area (3-D) (people per km²)	**8,635**

2-D Percentages		
Greenspace		**62%**
Agriculture	0%	
Lawn	0%	
Park	62%	
Wilderness	0%	
Water		**1%**
Infrastructure		**23%**
Built Area		**14%**
Housing	6%	
Industrial	0%	
Public	8%	
Total % of land use (can exceed 100%)		**100%**

3-D Percentages		
Greenspace		**36%**
Agriculture	0%	
Lawn	0%	
Park	36%	
Wilderness	0%	
Water		**1%**
Infrastructure		**13%**
Built Area		**50%**
Housing	40%	
Industrial	0%	
Public	10%	
Total % of land use		**100%**

Based largely on Shadrach Woods's "stem" architecture, the multi-functional urban complex at Toulouse Le Mirail was a massive manifestation and test of Team 10's ideas. The project created an entirely new portion of the city and featured housing, schools, as well as public and commercial buildings, and parkland. The spine of the project was to be a large pedestrian deck that would weave between the hexagonally-angled apartment towers. The deck, which was not built, was designed to separate car traffic from pedestrians, and access paths to the towers themselves would come off the "trunk" as branches in the pedestrian network.

2D DENSITY RANKING	FAR RANKING	GREENSPACE RANKING	POPULATION RANKING	3D DENSITY RANKING
17/49	22/49	22/49	25/49	14/49

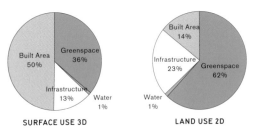

SURFACE USE 3D   LAND USE 2D

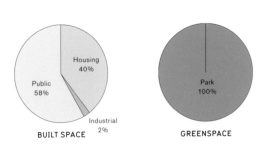

BUILT SPACE   GREENSPACE

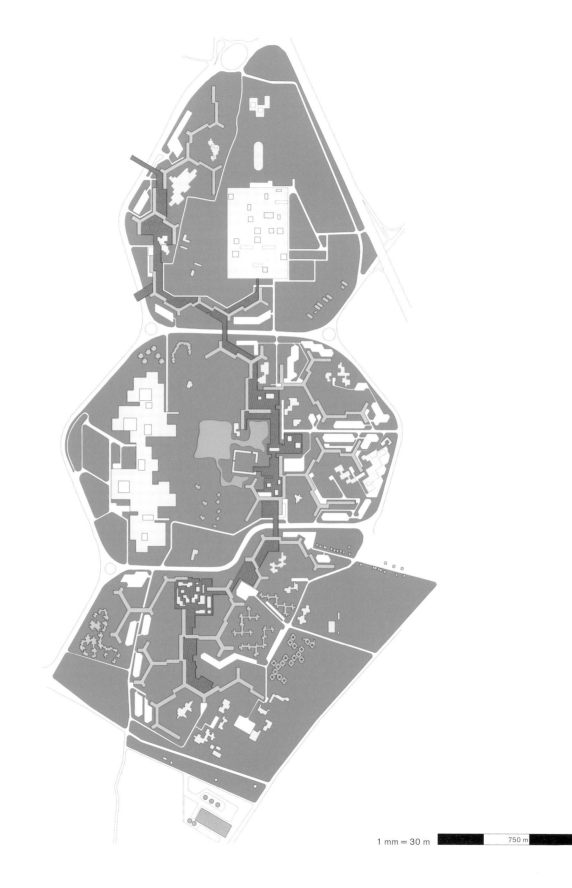

1 mm = 30 m   750 m   1500 m

BRIDGE-TOWN OVER THE CHANNEL

English Channel, UK, 1963
Yona Friedman and
Eckhardt Schultze-Fielitz

Total Site Area (2-D; in m²)	3,662,709

Total Greenspace (m²)	-
Area: Greenspace: agriculture	-
Area: Greenspace: lawn	-
Area: Greenspace: park	-
Area: Greenspace: wilderness	-

Area of Water (m²)	2,188,061
Area of Infrastructure (m²)	1,046,488

Total Built Area [footprint; m²)]	1,474,648
Area: Housing (footprint)	491,549
Area: Industrial (footprint)	491,549
Area: Public (footprint)	491,549

Total Population	30,000
Total number housing units	n/a
Number of people per housing unit	n/a

Total Area (3-D; in m²)	8,150,043
Number of Floors: Housing	3
Number of Floors: Industrial	4
Number of Floors: Public	3
Area: Total Built	4,915,494
Area: Housing (3-D)	1,474,648
Area: Industrial (3-D)	1,966,198
Area: Public (3-D)	1,474,648
Area: Open Space (Greenspace + Water + Infrastructure) (3-D)	3,234,549

FAR: 3-D Area / 2-D Area (x)	2.23

DENSITY: total population / site area (2-D) (people per km²)	8,191
DENSITY: total population / total area (3-D) (people per km²)	3,681

2-D Percentages		
Greenspace		0%
Agriculture	0%	
Lawn	0%	
Park	0%	
Wilderness	0%	
Water		60%
Infrastructure		29%
Built Area		40%
Housing	13%	
Industrial	13%	
Public	14%	
Total % of land use (can exceed 100%)		129%

3-D Percentages		
Greenspace		0%
Agriculture	0%	
Lawn	0%	
Park	0%	
Wilderness	0%	
Water		27%
Infrastructure		13%
Built Area		60%
Housing	18%	
Industrial	24%	
Public	18%	
Total % of land use		100%

A result of Eckhardt Schultze-Fielitz and Yona Friedman's experiments with space-frame structural systems, their proposal for a Bridge-Town spanning the English Channel was also in tune with the developing aesthetics of the Situationists. Friedman's earlier Spatial City schemes for Paris and New York, proposed a series of multi-functional units that could fill a megastructural space-frame hovering above an existing city. Similarly, in Bridge-Town over the Channel, a transport core is flanked by residential, commercial and industrial units that are inserted by inhabitants as needed. The essentially mercantile Bridge-Town features hotels and artificial beaches, has rail and highway infrastructures, and could accommodate ocean shipping in multiple ports.

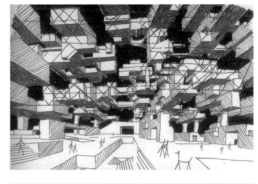

2D DENSITY RANKING	FAR RANKING	GREENSPACE RANKING	POPULATION RANKING	3D DENSITY RANKING
21/49	18/49	48/49	29/49	25/49

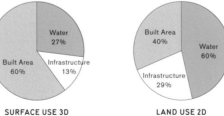

SURFACE USE 3D — Water 27%, Built Area 60%, Infrastructure 13%

LAND USE 2D — Built Area 40%, Water 60%, Infrastructure 29%

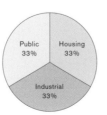

BUILT SPACE — Public 33%, Housing 33%, Industrial 33%

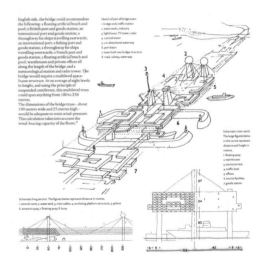

1 mm = 10 m ▇▇▇▇▇▇▇▇ 500 m

Total Site Area (2-D; in m²)	**53,376**

Total Greenspace (m²)	**2,600**
Area: Greenspace: agriculture	0
Area: Greenspace: lawn	0
Area: Greenspace: park	2,600
Area: Greenspace: wilderness	0

Area of Water (m²)	**0**
Area of Infrastructure (m²)	**5,338**

Total Built Area [footprint; m²)]	**53,376**
Area: Housing (footprint)	0
Area: Industrial (footprint)	0
Area: Public (footprint)	53,376

Total Population	**10,000**
Total number housing units	0
Number of people per housing unit	0

Total Area (3-D; in m²)	**221,442**
Number of Floors: Housing	0
Number of Floors: Industrial	0
Number of Floors: Public	4
Area: Total Built	**213,504**
Area: Housing (3-D)	-
Area: Industrial (3-D)	-
Area: Public (3-D)	213,504
Area: Open Space (Greenspace + Water + Infrastructure) (3-D)	7,938

FAR: 3-D Area / 2-D Area (x)	**4.15**

DENSITY: total population / site area (2-D) (people per km²)	**187,350**
DENSITY: total population / total area (3-D) (people per km²)	**45,159**

2-D Percentages	
Greenspace	**5%**
Agriculture	0%
Lawn	0%
Park	5%
Wilderness	0%
Water	**0%**
Infrastructure	**10%**
Built Area	**100%**
Housing	0%
Industrial	0%
Public	100%
Total % of land use (can exceed 100%)	**115%**

3-D Percentages	
Greenspace	**1%**
Agriculture	0%
Lawn	0%
Park	1%
Wilderness	0%
Water	**0%**
Infrastructure	**2%**
Built Area	**97%**
Housing	0%
Industrial	0%
Public	97%
Total % of land use	**100%**

This project for an urban infill by the Team 10–affiliated firm of Candilis-Josic-Woods–was to replace a bombed area in central Frankfurt. An early mat-building, the project was comprised of multiple platforms containing programmed structures, patios and streets. The web of platforms is interspersed with openings, allowing for the creation of buildings that inhabit multiple levels. The network would be flexible, and could continually be readapted by the city's inhabitants.

Views of the model from the west, the south and the east.

2D DENSITY RANKING	FAR RANKING	GREENSPACE RANKING	POPULATION RANKING	3D DENSITY RANKING
2/49	8/49	41/49	36/49	1/49*

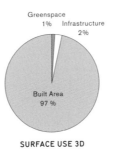

Greenspace 1% Infrastructure 2%
Built Area 97%

SURFACE USE 3D

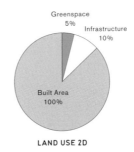

Greenspace 5% Infrastructure 10%
Built Area 100%

LAND USE 2D

Public 100%

BUILT SPACE

Park 100%

GREENSPACE

1 mm = 2 m ▮▮▮▮▮ 50 m ▮▮▮ 100 m

MOUND

United Kingdom, 1964
Peter Cook

Total Site Area (2-D; in m²)	**9,022**
Total Greenspace (m²)	**9,022**
Area: Greenspace: agriculture	0
Area: Greenspace: lawn	0
Area: Greenspace: park	0
Area: Greenspace: wilderness	9,022
Area of Water (m²)	**0**
Area of Infrastructure (m²)	**0**
Total Built Area [footprint; m²)]	**9,022**
Area: Housing (footprint)	0
Area: Industrial (footprint)	0
Area: Public (footprint)	9,022
Total Population	**60**
Total number housing units	0
Number of people per housing unit	0
Total Area (3-D; in m²)	**63,154**
Number of Floors: Housing	0
Number of Floors: Industrial	0
Number of Floors: Public	6
Area: Total Built	**54,132**
Area: Housing (3-D)	-
Area: Industrial (3-D)	-
Area: Public (3-D)	54,132
Area: Open Space (Greenspace + Water + Infrastructure) (3-D)	9,022
FAR: 3-D Area / 2-D Area (x)	**7.00**
DENSITY: total population / site area (2-D) (people per km²)	**6,650**
DENSITY: total population / total area (3-D) (people per km²)	**950**

2-D Percentages	
Greenspace	**100%**
Agriculture	0%
Lawn	0%
Park	0%
Wilderness	100%
Water	**0%**
Infrastructure	**100%**
Built Area	**100%**
Housing	0%
Industrial	0%
Public	100%
Total % of land use (can exceed 100%)	**300%**

3-D Percentages	
Greenspace	**14%**
Agriculture	0%
Lawn	0%
Park	0%
Wilderness	14%
Water	**0%**
Infrastructure	**0%**
Built Area	**86%**
Housing	0%
Industrial	0%
Public	86%
Total % of land use	**100%**

Mound, a proposal by Archigram's Peter Cook, is a multi-use center buried under a grassy hill. The project is sectionally stratified, and features recreation areas, a coffee shop, shopping malls, and an auditorium. It also contains a monorail station, linking it with the outside world.

Peter Cook, Mound, 1964
A multi-use centre, inward-looking and covered with grass banks.

2D DENSITY RANKING	FAR RANKING	GREENSPACE RANKING	POPULATION RANKING	3D DENSITY RANKING
24/49	3/49	2/49	49/49	42/49

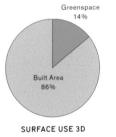

SURFACE USE 3D

Greenspace 14%
Built Area 86%

LAND USE 2D

Built Area 100%
Greenspace 100%
Infrastructure 100%

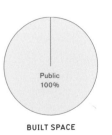

BUILT SPACE

Public 100%

GREENSPACE

Wilderness 100%

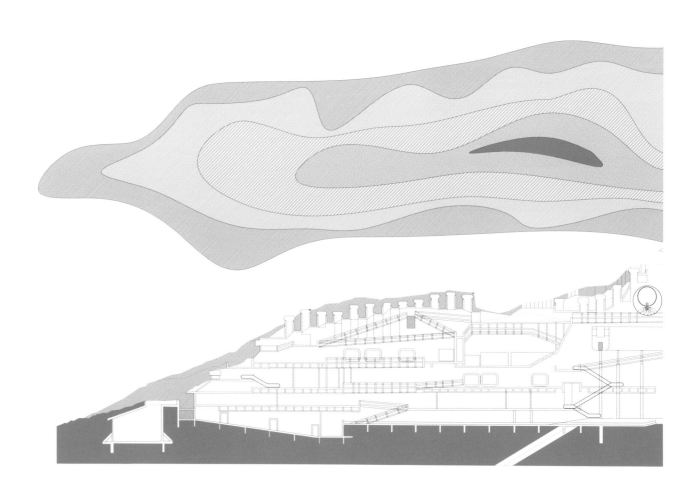

United Kingdom, 1964
Archigram

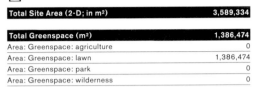

Total Site Area (2-D; in m²)	**3,589,334**

Total Greenspace (m²)	**1,386,474**
Area: Greenspace: agriculture	0
Area: Greenspace: lawn	1,386,474
Area: Greenspace: park	0
Area: Greenspace: wilderness	0

Area of Water (m²)	**0**
Area of Infrastructure (m²)	**836,656**

Total Built Area [footprint; m²)]	**1,366,204**
Area: Housing (footprint)	66,720
Area: Industrial (footprint)	212,224
Area: Public (footprint)	1,087,260

Total Population	**355000**
Total number housing units	672
Number of people per housing unit	

Total Area (3-D; in m²)	**9,995,906**
Number of Floors: Housing	6
Number of Floors: Industrial	4
Number of Floors: Public	6
Area: Total Built	**7,772,776**
Area: Housing (3-D)	400,320
Area: Industrial (3-D)	848,896
Area: Public (3-D)	6,523,560
Area: Open Space (Greenspace + Water + Infrastructure) (3-D)	2,223,130

FAR: 3-D Area / 2-D Area (x)	**2.78**

DENSITY: total population / site area (2-D) (people per km²)	**98,904**
DENSITY: total population / total area (3-D) (people per km²)	**35,515**

2-D Percentages		
Greenspace		**39%**
Agriculture	0%	
Lawn	39%	
Park	0%	
Wilderness	0%	
Water		**0%**
Infrastructure		**23%**
Built Area		**38%**
Housing	2%	
Industrial	6%	
Public	30%	
Total % of land use (can exceed 100%)		**100%**

3-D Percentages		
Greenspace		**14%**
Agriculture	0%	
Lawn	14%	
Park	0%	
Wilderness	0%	
Water		**0%**
Infrastructure		**8%**
Built Area		**78%**
Housing	4%	
Industrial	8%	
Public	66%	
Total % of land use		**100%**

Archigram's best-known project, Plug-in City was to be a giant, highly adaptable diagrid space-frame megastructure. The different sections of the project, which included residential towers, office structures, honeycomb theaters, and information silos, were to be connected by communication pipes. Each structure was to have cranes on top, with which the individual modules comprising the different functions could be easily moved and exchanged. The plan placed the structural grid on a 45-degree angle to a monorail route that was to connect existing cities; alongside ran a giant route for hovercraft. Removable roads, railways, and public spaces covered by inflatable roofs in bad weather were to hang from the superstructure.

2D DENSITY RANKING	FAR RANKING	GREENSPACE RANKING	POPULATION RANKING	3D DENSITY RANKING
5/49	11/49	30/49	14/49	3/49

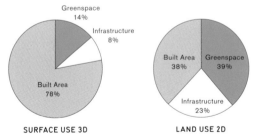

SURFACE USE 3D

LAND USE 2D

BUILT SPACE

GREENSPACE

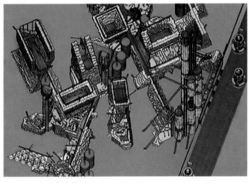

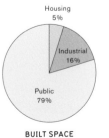

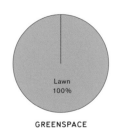

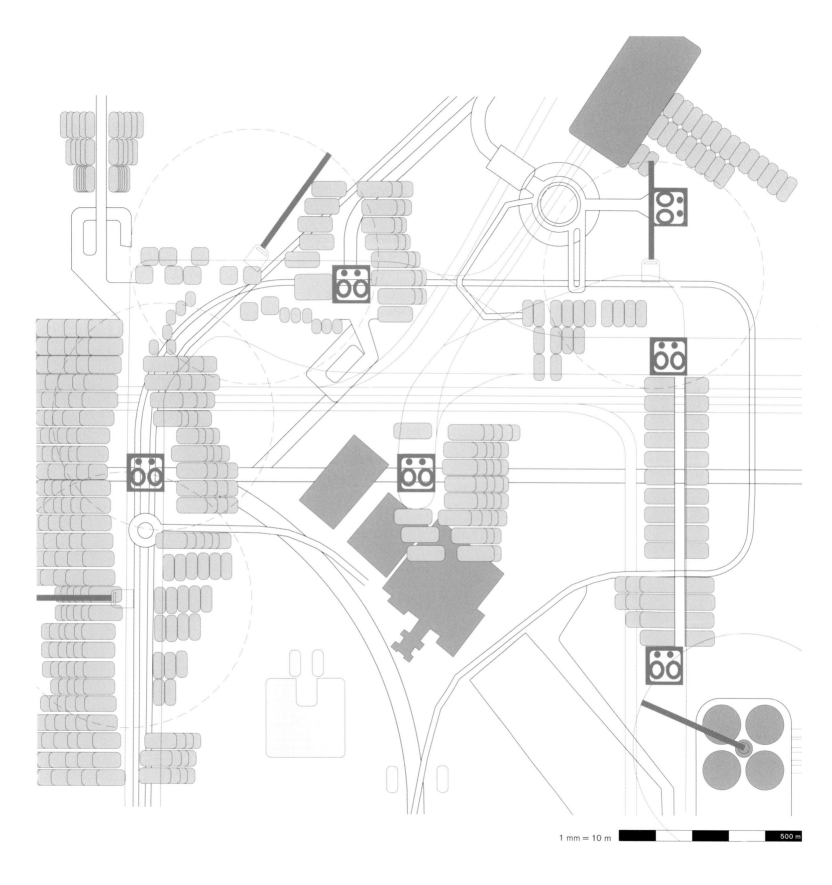

1 mm = 10 m ▰▰▰▰ 500 m

FUN PALACE

England, 1965
Cedric Price

Total Site Area (2-D; in m²)	15,909

Total Greenspace (m²)	0
Area: Greenspace: agriculture	0
Area: Greenspace: lawn	0
Area: Greenspace: park	0
Area: Greenspace: wilderness	

Area of Water (m²)	0
Area of Infrastructure (m²)	15,909

Total Built Area [footprint; m²)]	15,909
Area: Housing (footprint)	0
Area: Industrial (footprint)	0
Area: Public (footprint)	15909

Total Population	2000
Total number housing units	
Number of people per housing unit	

Total Area (3-D; in m²)	95,454
Number of Floors: Housing	0
Number of Floors: Industrial	0
Number of Floors: Public	5
Area: Total Built	79,545
Area: Housing (3-D)	0
Area: Industrial (3-D)	0
Area: Public (3-D)	79,545
Area: Open Space (Greenspace + Water + Infrastructure) (3-D)	15,909

FAR: 3-D Area / 2-D Area (x)	6.00

DENSITY: total population / site area (2-D) (people per km²)	125,715
DENSITY: total population / total area (3-D) (people per km²)	20,953

2-D Percentages	
Greenspace	0%
Agriculture	0%
Lawn	0%
Park	0%
Wilderness	0%
Water	0%
Infrastructure	100%
Built Area	100%
Housing	0%
Industrial	0%
Public	100%
Total % of land use (can exceed 100%)	200%

3-D Percentages	
Greenspace	0%
Agriculture	0%
Lawn	0%
Park	0%
Wilderness	0%
Water	0%
Infrastructure	17%
Built Area	83%
Housing	0%
Industrial	0%
Public	83%
Total % of land use	100%

A megastructure whose primary function was improvised public performance, the Fun Palace featured facilities for dancing, music, drama, and fireworks. The seven-acre unenclosed steel structure would be fully serviced by traveling gantry cranes. Accessible only by air or water, the temporary structure would allow for 55,000 visitors. The Fun Palace was to be inherently flexible, with only the 3-D grid as a fixed component, and in fact was designed as a series of architectural "performances" as the building transformed. Although never built, the scheme is widely considered to have been influential in the design of the Centre Georges Pompidou.

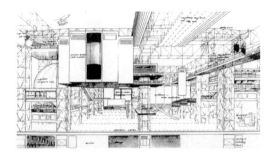

2D DENSITY RANKING	FAR RANKING	GREENSPACE RANKING	POPULATION RANKING	3D DENSITY RANKING
3/49	4/49	47/49	42/49	7/49

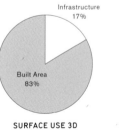

SURFACE USE 3D

LAND USE 2D

BUILT SPACE

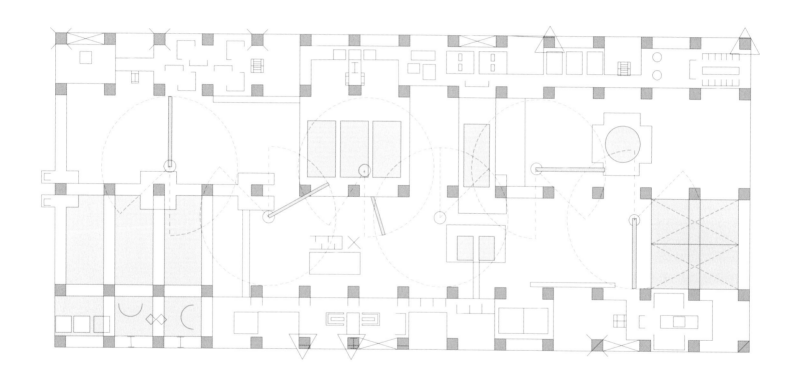

1 mm = 1 m ▮▮▮▮▮ 25 m ▮▮▮▮▮ 50 m

RATINGEN-WEST

Dusseldorf, Germany, 1965
Merete Mattern

Total Site Area (2-D; in m²)	**6,457,015**
Total Greenspace (m²)	**5,160,000**
Area: Greenspace: agriculture	0
Area: Greenspace: lawn	4,128,000
Area: Greenspace: park	1,032,000
Area: Greenspace: wilderness	0
Area of Water (m²)	**0**
Area of Infrastructure (m²)	**232,850**
Total Built Area [footprint; m²)]	**1,064,165**
Area: Housing (footprint)	1,064,165
Area: Industrial (footprint)	0
Area: Public (footprint)	0
Total Population	**14,000**
Total number housing units	~3500
Number of people per housing unit	4.0
Total Area (3-D; in m²)	**14,970,335**
Number of Floors: Housing	9
Number of Floors: Industrial	0
Number of Floors: Public	0
Area: Total Built	**9,577,485**
Area: Housing (3-D)	9,577,485
Area: Industrial (3-D)	0
Area: Public (3-D)	0
Area: Open Space (Greenspace + Water + Infrastructure) (3-D)	5,392,850
FAR: 3-D Area / 2-D Area (x)	**2.32**
DENSITY: total population / site area (2-D) (people per km²)	**2,168**
DENSITY: total population / total area (3-D) (people per km²)	**935**

2-D Percentages

Greenspace		**80%**
	Agriculture	0%
	Lawn	64%
	Park	16%
	Wilderness	0%
Water		**0%**
Infrastructure		**4%**
Built Area		**16%**
	Housing	16%
	Industrial	0%
	Public	0%
Total % of land use (can exceed 100%)		**100%**

3-D Percentages

Greenspace		**34%**
	Agriculture	0%
	Lawn	27%
	Park	7%
	Wilderness	0%
Water		**0%**
Infrastructure		**2%**
Built Area		**64%**
	Housing	64%
	Industrial	0%
	Public	0%
Total % of land use		**100%**

The Ratingen West project, a competition entry by Merete Mattern, proposed a multi-functional expansion of Dusseldorf. Praised by Sibyl Moholy-Nagy her book *Matrix of Man*, Ratingen was organized in deference to its hilly landscape, creating an almost picturesque assemblage of towers and terraced housing. The project was part of a movement among megastructural proposals to utilize naturalistic forms and patterns in their plans.

SECTION THROUGH RESIDENTIAL COMPLEX WITH TERRACE HOUSES

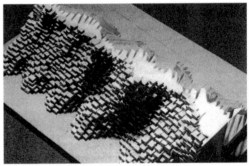

2D DENSITY RANKING	FAR RANKING	GREENSPACE RANKING	POPULATION RANKING	3D DENSITY RANKING
42/49	16/49	14/49	35/49	43/49

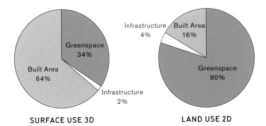

SURFACE USE 3D   LAND USE 2D

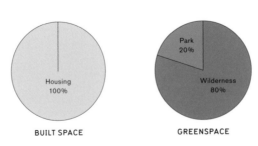

BUILT SPACE   GREENSPACE

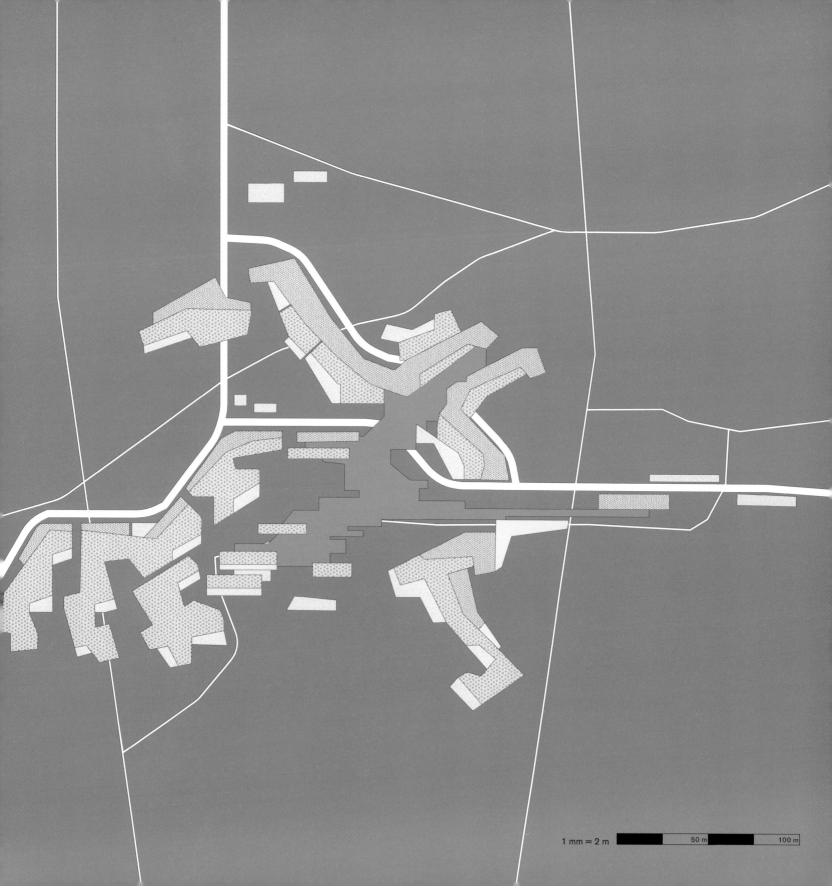

1 mm = 2 m ■■■■■■■■■■ 50 m ■■■■■■■■■■ 100 m

SATELLITE CITY

Principality of Monaco, 1965
Manfredo Nicoletti

Total Site Area (2-D; in m²)	**3,143,875**
Total Greenspace (m²)	**1,224,851**
Area: Greenspace: agriculture	0
Area: Greenspace: lawn	9,537
Area: Greenspace: park	359,816
Area: Greenspace: wilderness	855497.8567
Area of Water (m²)	**1,228,546**
Area of Infrastructure (m²)	**396,589**
Total Built Area [footprint; m²)]	**293,889**
Area: Housing (footprint)	108,739
Area: Industrial (footprint)	64,656
Area: Public (footprint)	120,494
Total Population	**22000**
Total number housing units	6090
Number of people per housing unit	3.61
Total Area (3-D; in m²)	**8,691,673**
Number of Floors: Housing	40
Number of Floors: Industrial	8
Number of Floors: Public	8
Area: Total Built	**5,830,755**
Area: Housing (3-D)	4,349,555
Area: Industrial (3-D)	517,244
Area: Public (3-D)	963,956
Area: Open Space (Greenspace + Water + Infrastructure) (3-D)	2,849,986
FAR: 3-D Area / 2-D Area (x)	**2.76**
DENSITY: total population / site area (2-D) (people per km²)	**6,998**
DENSITY: total population / total area (3-D) (people per km²)	**2,534**

2-D Percentages		
Greenspace		**39%**
Agriculture	0%	
Lawn	0%	
Park	11%	
Wilderness	28%	
Water		**39%**
Infrastructure		**13%**
Built Area		**9%**
Housing	3%	
Industrial	2%	
Public	4%	
Total % of land use (can exceed 100%)		**100%**

3-D Percentages		
Greenspace		**14%**
Agriculture	0%	
Lawn	0%	
Park	4%	
Wilderness	10%	
Water		**14%**
Infrastructure		**5%**
Built Area		**67%**
Housing	46%	
Industrial	7%	
Public	14%	
Total % of land use		**100%**

Nicoletti's complex expands the existing city-state of Monaco into the sea, using landfill. The semi-circular terraced amphitheaters contain housing while parks, along with port functions, are situated at water level. Circulation and commerce takes place along enclosed roads and shopping promenades on multiple levels. Greenspace is also found throughout the different levels of the project, with many residences having large terraces.

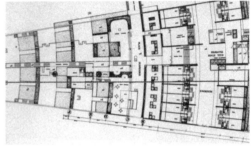

2D DENSITY RANKING	FAR RANKING	GREENSPACE RANKING	POPULATION RANKING	3D DENSITY RANKING
23/49	**12/49**	**29/49**	**32/49**	**29/49**

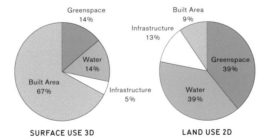

SURFACE USE 3D
LAND USE 2D

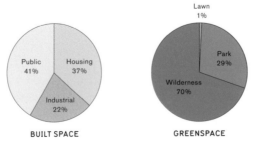

BUILT SPACE
GREENSPACE

1 mm = 5 m   125 m   250 m

Total Site Area (2-D; in m²)	4,486,024

Total Greenspace (m²)	2,768,724
Area: Greenspace: agriculture	0
Area: Greenspace: lawn	
Area: Greenspace: park	2768724.04
Area: Greenspace: wilderness	0

Area of Water (m²)	0
Area of Infrastructure (m²)	366366

Total Built Area [footprint; m²)]	4,600,556
Area: Housing (footprint)	1,831,832
Area: Industrial (footprint)	0
Area: Public (footprint)	2,768,724

Total Population	1,000,000
Total number housing units	300,000
Number of people per housing unit	3.3

Total Area (3-D; in m²)	252,246,346
Number of Floors: Housing	200
Number of Floors: Industrial	0
Number of Floors: Public	4
Area: Total Built	249,111,255
Area: Housing (3-D)	241,801,824
Area: Industrial (3-D)	0
Area: Public (3-D)	7,309,431
Area: Open Space (Greenspace + Water + Infrastructure) (3-D)	3,135,090

FAR: 3-D Area / 2-D Area (x)	56.23

DENSITY: total population / site area (2-D) (people per km²)	222,915
DENSITY: total population / total area (3-D) (people per km²)	3,964

2-D Percentages	
Greenspace	61%
Agriculture	0%
Lawn	0%
Park	61%
Wilderness	0%
Water	0%
Infrastructure	8%
Built Area	103%
Housing	41%
Industrial	0%
Public	62%
Total % of land use (can exceed 100%)	172%

3-D Percentages	
Greenspace	1%
Agriculture	0%
Lawn	0%
Park	1%
Wilderness	0%
Water	0%
Infrastructure	0%
Built Area	99%
Housing	96%
Industrial	0%
Public	3%
Total % of land use	100%

Proposed by Buckminster Fuller for multiple locations, including San Francisco and Tokyo, Tetrahedral City was to be a floating or land-based residential pyramid that could grow to accommodate one million inhabitants. The building was to have three triangular walls for a total of 300,000 living units, 200-stories tall with two-mile long walls at its base. Large openings in the structure would occur every fifty stories, allowing sunlight to enter the public garden at the bottom of the interior. Three city centers would rim the structure at different levels. Each of these featured "a community park, complete with lagoon, palms and shopping center in geodesic domes." Fuller employed the tetrahedron shape due to its having the most surface per volume area of all polyhedra, and therefore its ability to provide the most living space with full access to the outdoors.

2D DENSITY RANKING	FAR RANKING	GREENSPACE RANKING	POPULATION RANKING	3D DENSITY RANKING
1/49*	1/49*	23/49	9/49	23/49

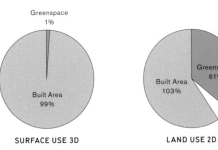

SURFACE USE 3D

Greenspace 1%
Built Area 99%

LAND USE 2D

Greenspace 61%
Built Area 103%
Infrastructure 8%

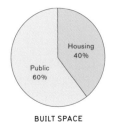

BUILT SPACE

Public 60%
Housing 40%

GREENSPACE

Park 100%

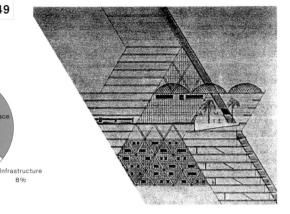

1 mm = 35 m   875 m   1750 m

New York, USA, 1967
McMillan, Griffis & Mileto

Total Site Area (2-D; in m²)	**2,027,940**
Total Greenspace (m²)	**311,997**
Area: Greenspace: agriculture	-
Area: Greenspace: lawn	150,000
Area: Greenspace: park	161,997
Area: Greenspace: wilderness	-
Area of Water (m²)	-
Area of Infrastructure (m²)	**832,480**
Total Built Area [footprint; m²)]	**883,463**
Area: Housing (footprint)	770,847
Area: Industrial (footprint)	-
Area: Public (footprint)	112,616
Total Population	**50,000**
Total number housing units	
Number of people per housing unit	
Total Area (3-D; in m²)	**6,350,106**
Number of Floors: Housing	5
Number of Floors: Industrial	
Number of Floors: Public	12
Area: Total Built	**5,205,629**
Area: Housing (3-D)	3,854,235
Area: Industrial (3-D)	-
Area: Public (3-D)	1,351,394
Area: Open Space (Greenspace + Water + Infrastructure) (3-D)	1,144,477
FAR: 3-D Area / 2-D Area (x)	**3.13**
DENSITY: total population / site area (2-D) (people per km²)	**24,656**
DENSITY: total population / total area (3-D) (people per km²)	**7,874**

2-D Percentages		
Greenspace		**15%**
Agriculture	0%	
Lawn	7%	
Park	8%	
Wilderness	0%	
Water		**0%**
Infrastructure		**41%**
Built Area		**44%**
Housing	38%	
Industrial	0%	
Public	6%	
Total % of land use (can exceed 100%)		**100%**

3-D Percentages		
Greenspace		**5%**
Agriculture	0%	
Lawn	2%	
Park	3%	
Wilderness	0%	
Water		**0%**
Infrastructure		**13%**
Built Area		**82%**
Housing	61%	
Industrial	0%	
Public	21%	
Total % of land use		**100%**

This scheme utilized the air rights over the proposed (and never built) Cross-Brooklyn Expressway to build a megastructural linear city. The plan included housing and office space, and connected to the existing urban fabric at multiple points. Like many multi-layer megastructure projects of the time, its section was pyramid-shaped, resulting in a series of terraced dwellings with a green pedestrian corridor over multiple layers of infrastructure and transport. Its failure to be realized was lamented by Ada Louise Huxtable in the *New York Times*.

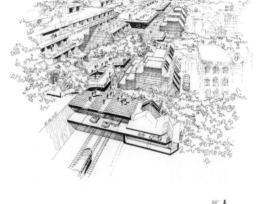

2D DENSITY RANKING	FAR RANKING	GREENSPACE RANKING	POPULATION RANKING	3D DENSITY RANKING
13/49	**9/49**	**39/49**	**24/49**	**16/49**

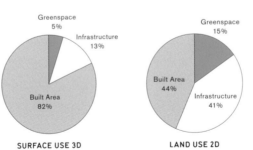

SURFACE USE 3D

LAND USE 2D

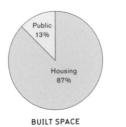

BUILT SPACE

GREENSPACE

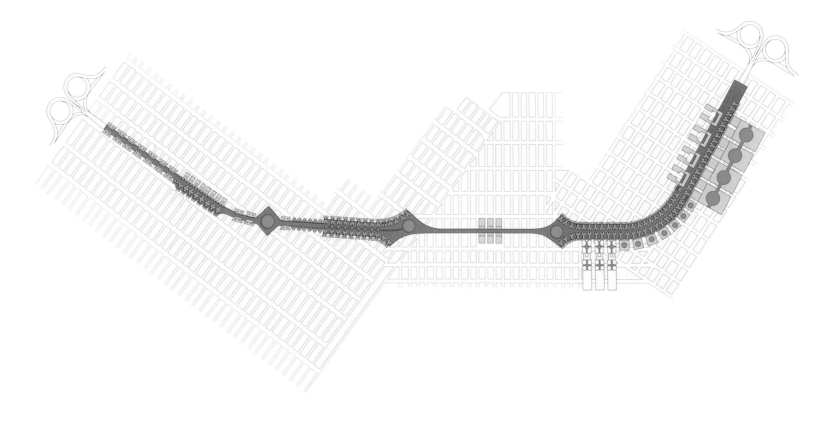

1 mm = 40 m   1 km   2 km

CONTINUOUS MONUMENT

Global, 1969
Superstudio

Total Site Area (2-D; in m²)	**11,856,518**
Total Greenspace (m²)	**2,964,130**
Area: Greenspace: agriculture	741,032
Area: Greenspace: lawn	741,032
Area: Greenspace: park	741,032
Area: Greenspace: wilderness	741,032
Area of Water (m²)	**2,964,130**
Area of Infrastructure (m²)	**2,964,130**
Total Built Area [footprint; m²)]	**2,964,130**
Area: Housing (footprint)	988,043
Area: Industrial (footprint)	988,043
Area: Public (footprint)	988,043
Total Population	**1,000,000**
Total number housing units	122,400
Number of people per housing unit	8.17
Total Area (3-D; in m²)	**32,605,425**
Number of Floors: Housing	8
Number of Floors: Industrial	8
Number of Floors: Public	8
Area: Total Built	**23,713,036**
Area: Housing (3-D)	7,904,345
Area: Industrial (3-D)	7,904,345
Area: Public (3-D)	7,904,345
Area: Open Space (Greenspace + Water + Infrastructure) (3-D)	8,892,389
FAR: 3-D Area / 2-D Area (x)	**2.75**
DENSITY: total population / site area (2-D) (people per km²)	**84,342**
DENSITY: total population / total area (3-D) (people per km²)	**30,670**

2-D Percentages		
Greenspace		**25%**
Agriculture	6%	
Lawn	6%	
Park	6%	
Wilderness	7%	
Water		**25%**
Infrastructure		**25%**
Built Area		**25%**
Housing	8%	
Industrial	8%	
Public	9%	
Total % of land use (can exceed 100%)		**100%**

3-D Percentages		
Greenspace		**9%**
Agriculture	2%	
Lawn	2%	
Park	2%	
Wilderness	3%	
Water		**9%**
Infrastructure		**9%**
Built Area		**73%**
Housing	24%	
Industrial	24%	
Public	25%	
Total % of land use		**100%**

The Continuous Monument was a reaction to the pop culture and hyper-saturated projects of the 1960s by the Italian "radical architecture" group Superstudio. The earth-spanning gridded network made of indeterminate material was to contain the entire human population and to connect the key expressions of humanity around the world—large monuments like the Colosseum, the Kaaba and the Taj Mahal. In a flippant retort to both Modernism and megastructural architecture, the infinite grid extends and undermines the supposedly rational systems of Le Corbusier and the International Style. Here, as the grid runs through Manhattan, bits of the existing city are surrounded and treated as historical artifacts in a museum-like setting.

2D DENSITY RANKING	FAR RANKING	GREENSPACE RANKING	POPULATION RANKING	3D DENSITY RANKING
6/49	13/49	34/49	10/49	5/49

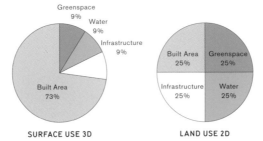

SURFACE USE 3D

Greenspace 9%
Water 9%
Infrastructure 9%
Built Area 73%

LAND USE 2D

Built Area 25%
Greenspace 25%
Infrastructure 25%
Water 25%

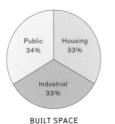

BUILT SPACE

Public 34%
Housing 33%
Industrial 33%

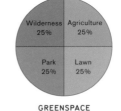

GREENSPACE

Wilderness 25%
Agriculture 25%
Park 25%
Lawn 25%

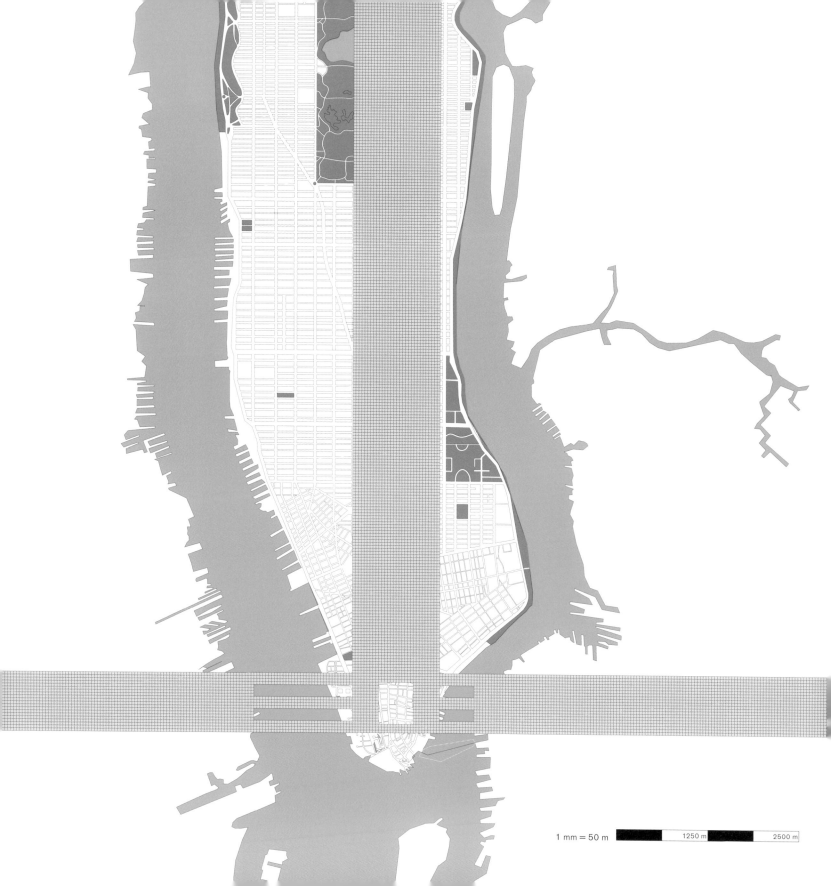

1 mm = 50 m   1250 m   2500 m

NO-STOP CITY

Global, 1969
Archizoom

Total Site Area (2-D; in m²)	478,457

Total Greenspace (m²)	437,406
Area: Greenspace: agriculture	11,089
Area: Greenspace: lawn	0
Area: Greenspace: park	50,744
Area: Greenspace: wilderness	375,572

Area of Water (m²)	0
Area of Infrastructure (m²)	60,921

Total Built Area [footprint; m²)]	81,618
Area: Housing (footprint)	27,206
Area: Industrial (footprint)	27,206
Area: Public (footprint)	27,206

Total Population	20,000
Total number housing units	9
Number of people per housing unit	2,222.22

Total Area (3-D; in m²)	852,005
Number of Floors: Housing	5
Number of Floors: Industrial	4
Number of Floors: Public	4
Area: Total Built	353,678
Area: Housing (3-D)	136,030
Area: Industrial (3-D)	108,824
Area: Public (3-D)	108,824
Area: Open Space (Greenspace + Water + Infrastructure) (3-D)	498,327

FAR: 3-D Area / 2-D Area (x)	1.78

DENSITY: total population / site area (2-D) (people per km²)	41,801
DENSITY: total population / total area (3-D) (people per km²)	23,474

2-D Percentages	
Greenspace	91%
Agriculture	2%
Lawn	0%
Park	11%
Wilderness	78%
Water	0%
Infrastructure	13%
Built Area	17%
Housing	6%
Industrial	6%
Public	5%
Total % of land use (can exceed 100%)	121%

3-D Percentages	
Greenspace	51%
Agriculture	1%
Lawn	0%
Park	6%
Wilderness	44%
Water	0%
Infrastructure	7%
Built Area	42%
Housing	16%
Industrial	13%
Public	13%
Total % of land use	100%

Archizoom Associates' No-Stop City, proposed around the same time as Superstudio's Continuous Monument, was also a reaction to, and a hyper-logical extension of, rational, consumer-driven design. Archizoom radically questioned the traditional status and function of design by proposing an infinitely tileable pattern of anonymous structures. Modeled on the supermarket, the factory, and the interior office environments of Büro Landschaft, No-Stop City was envisioned as a "well-equipped residential parking lot" composed of "large floors, micro-climatized and artificially lighted interiors." Without an exterior, these "potentially limitless urban structures" could be "made uniform through climate control and made optimal by information links." Rather than serving to identify a place, No-Stop City would be a neutral field in which the creation of identity through consumption could be unfettered.

2D DENSITY RANKING	FAR RANKING	GREENSPACE RANKING	POPULATION RANKING	3D DENSITY RANKING
8/49	20/49	8/49	34/49	6/49

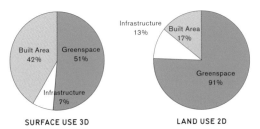

SURFACE USE 3D

LAND USE 2D

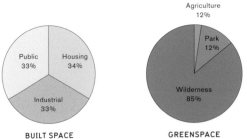

BUILT SPACE

GREENSPACE

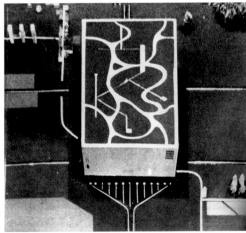

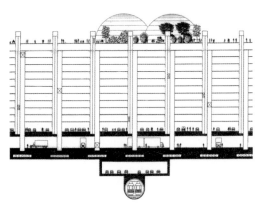

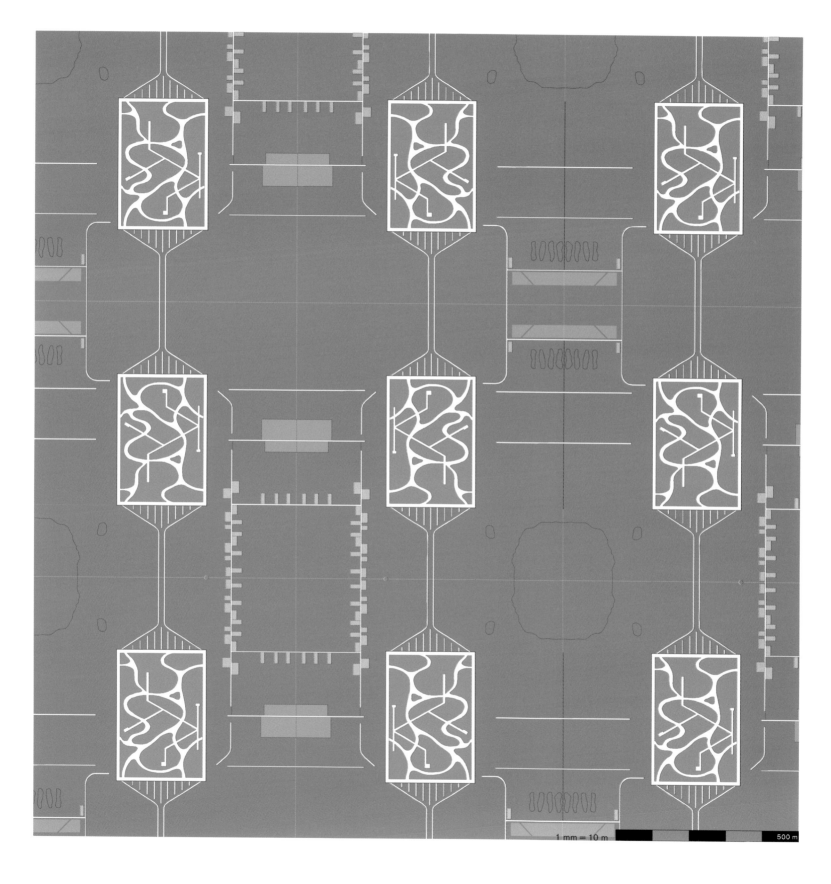

1 mm = 10 m   500 m

NOAHBABEL

Coastal waters, 1969
Paolo Soleri

Total Site Area (2-D; in m²)	**3,459,858**
Total Greenspace (m²)	**204,933**
Area: Greenspace: agriculture	0
Area: Greenspace: lawn	0
Area: Greenspace: park	204,933
Area: Greenspace: wilderness	0
Area of Water (m²)	**1,452,510**
Area of Infrastructure (m²)	**1,166,342**
Total Built Area [footprint; m²)]	**841,006**
Area: Housing (footprint)	344,813
Area: Industrial (footprint)	159,791
Area: Public (footprint)	336,402
Total Population	**90,000**
Total number housing units	30,000
Number of people per housing unit	3.00
Total Area (3-D; in m²)	**17,505,755**
Number of Floors: Housing	30
Number of Floors: Industrial	8
Number of Floors: Public	9
Area: Total Built	**14,683,969**
Area: Housing (3-D)	10,344,377
Area: Industrial (3-D)	1,278,329
Area: Public (3-D)	3,061,263
Area: Open Space (Greenspace + Water + Infrastructure) (3-D)	2,823,786
FAR: 3-D Area / 2-D Area (x)	**5.06**
DENSITY: total population / site area (2-D) (people per km²)	**26,013**
DENSITY: total population / total area (3-D) (people per km²)	**5,141**

2-D Percentages	
Greenspace	**6%**
Agriculture	0%
Lawn	0%
Park	6%
Wilderness	0%
Water	**42%**
Infrastructure	**34%**
Built Area	**24%**
Housing	10%
Industrial	5%
Public	10%
Total % of land use (can exceed 100%)	**106%**

3-D Percentages	
Greenspace	**1%**
Agriculture	0%
Lawn	0%
Park	1%
Wilderness	0%
Water	**8%**
Infrastructure	**7%**
Built Area	**84%**
Housing	59%
Industrial	7%
Public	18%
Total % of land use	**100%**

Noahbabel, one of Paolo Soleri's Arcology projects, followed the design principles laid out in his book *The City in the Image of Man*. These principles called for a hyperdense city designed to maximize human interaction and access to shared cost-effective infrastructural services like water and sewage. The Arcologies proposed in the book attempt to minimize the use of energy, raw materials and land; reduce waste and pollution; and allow interaction with the surrounding natural environment. Noahbabel, an aquatic Arcology, features apartments and residences near vertical cores of structure, and is rigidly zoned into work, housing, leisure, and transportation functions.

2D DENSITY RANKING	FAR RANKING	GREENSPACE RANKING	POPULATION RANKING	3D DENSITY RANKING
12/49	**6/49**	**40/49**	**20/49**	**18/49**

SURFACE USE 3D — Greenspace 1%, Infrastructure 7%, Water 8%, Built Area 84%

LAND USE 2D — Greenspace 6%, Built Area 24%, Water 42%, Infrastructure 34%

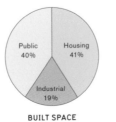

BUILT SPACE — Public 40%, Housing 41%, Industrial 19%

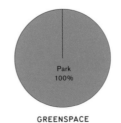

GREENSPACE — Park 100%

1

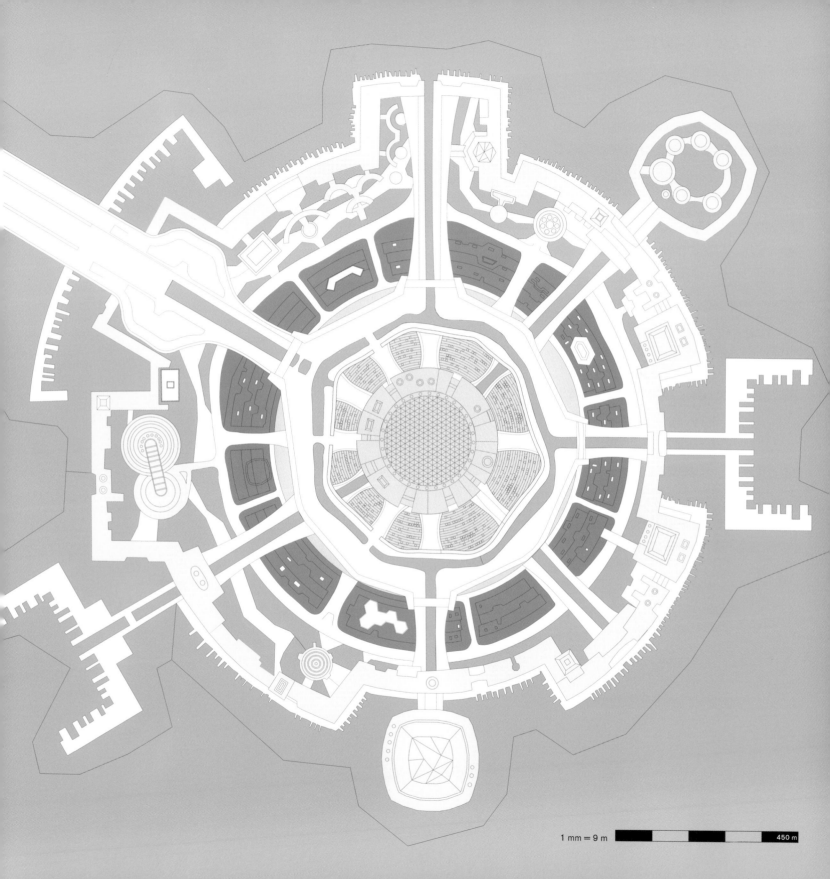

1 mm = 9 m ▮▮▮▮▮▮▮ 450 m

Total Site Area (2-D; in m²)	**2,160,000**

Total Greenspace (m²)	**1,628,212**
Area: Greenspace: agriculture	31,541
Area: Greenspace: lawn	48,438
Area: Greenspace: park	17,150
Area: Greenspace: wilderness	1,531,083

Area of Water (m²)	**0**
Area of Infrastructure (m²)	**496,976**

Total Built Area [footprint; m²)]	**107,740**
Area: Housing (footprint)	104,437
Area: Industrial (footprint)	0
Area: Public (footprint)	3,303

Total Population	**1,872**
Total number housing units	624
Number of people per housing unit	3.00

Total Area (3-D; in m²)	**2,232,928**
Number of Floors: Housing	1
Number of Floors: Industrial	1
Number of Floors: Public	1
Area: Total Built	**107,740**
Area: Housing (3-D)	104,437
Area: Industrial (3-D)	0
Area: Public (3-D)	3,303
Area: Open Space (Greenspace + Water + Infrastructure) (3-D)	2,125,188

FAR: 3-D Area / 2-D Area (x)	**1.03**

DENSITY: total population / site area (2-D) (people per km²)	**867**
DENSITY: total population / total area (3-D) (people per km²)	**838**

2-D Percentages		
Greenspace		**75%**
Agriculture	1%	
Lawn	2%	
Park	1%	
Wilderness	71%	
Water		**0%**
Infrastructure		**23%**
Built Area		**5%**
Housing	5%	
Industrial	0%	
Public	0%	
Total % of land use (can exceed 100%)		**103%**

3-D Percentages		
Greenspace		**73%**
Agriculture	1%	
Lawn	2%	
Park	1%	
Wilderness	69%	
Water		**0%**
Infrastructure		**22%**
Built Area		**5%**
Housing	5%	
Industrial	0%	
Public	0%	
Total % of land use		**100%**

Earthships were an idea for environmentally-oriented living proposed by Mike Reynolds. The project defined the home as a sustainable ecosystem, with indigenous and reused materials used for construction. Off-grid, and able to generate their own utilities, the Earthships were U-shaped homes utilizing high thermal mass walls made from used automobile tires filled with rammed earth. Other environmental technologies used in the project included rainwater collection, gray-water reuse, photovoltaic cells, and passive solar heating and cooling. The Earthships would form an agglomeration of artificial hills to create a settlement.

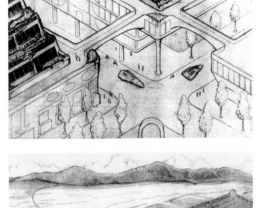

2D DENSITY RANKING	FAR RANKING	GREENSPACE RANKING	POPULATION RANKING	3D DENSITY RANKING
46/49	**45/49**	**15/49**	**44/49**	**44/49**

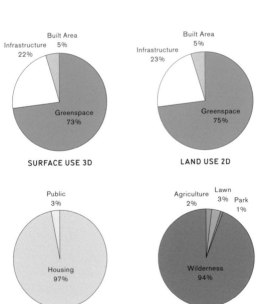

Built Area 5%
Infrastructure 22%
Greenspace 73%
SURFACE USE 3D

Built Area 5%
Infrastructure 23%
Greenspace 75%
LAND USE 2D

Public 3%
Housing 97%
BUILT SPACE

Agriculture 2% — Lawn 3% — Park 1%
Wilderness 94%
GREENSPACE

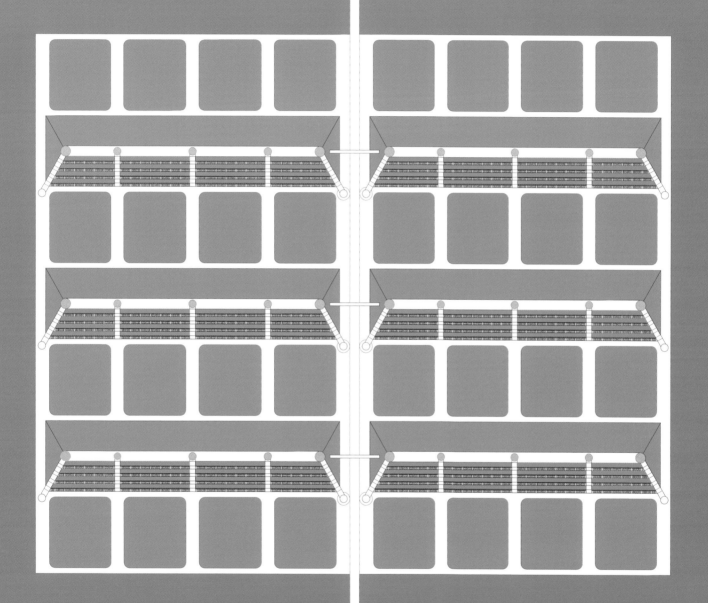

1 mm = 5 m   125 m   250 m

CONVENTION CITY

Houston, Texas, USA, 1972
Ant Farm

Total Site Area (2-D; in m²)	**4,687,975**

Total Greenspace (m²)	**4,441,060**
Area: Greenspace: agriculture	0
Area: Greenspace: lawn	0
Area: Greenspace: park	1,709
Area: Greenspace: wilderness	4,439,351

Area of Water (m²)	**0**
Area of Infrastructure (m²)	**102,108**

Total Built Area [footprint; m²)]	**196,605**
Area: Housing (footprint)	51,799
Area: Industrial (footprint)	0
Area: Public (footprint)	144,806

Total Population	**20,000**
Total number housing units	13,333
Number of people per housing unit	1.50

Total Area (3-D; in m²)	**4,884,580**
Number of Floors: Housing	1
Number of Floors: Industrial	0
Number of Floors: Public	2
Area: Total Built	**341,412**
Area: Housing (3-D)	51,799
Area: Industrial (3-D)	0
Area: Public (3-D)	289,613
Area: Open Space (Greenspace + Water + Infrastructure) (3-D)	4,543,169

FAR: 3-D Area / 2-D Area (x)	**1.04**

DENSITY: total population / site area (2-D) (people per km²)	**4,266**
DENSITY: total population / total area (3-D) (people per km²)	**4,095**

2-D Percentages	
Greenspace	**95%**
Agriculture	0%
Lawn	0%
Park	0%
Wilderness	95%
Water	**0%**
Infrastructure	**2%**
Built Area	**4%**
Housing	1%
Industrial	0%
Public	3%
Total % of land use (can exceed 100%)	**101%**

3-D Percentages	
Greenspace	**91%**
Agriculture	0%
Lawn	0%
Park	0%
Wilderness	91%
Water	**0%**
Infrastructure	**2%**
Built Area	**7%**
Housing	1%
Industrial	0%
Public	6%
Total % of land use	**100%**

Ant Farm's Convention City project, proposed in anticipation of the American bicentennial celebrations of 1976, features a bubble-enclosed convention center flanked by residential units. The apartments were to look down on the "open air" convention center, a lake, and communication towers, which would be used to relay convention activities on television. The football-field sized convention floor in the shape of the US is covered in artificial grass, and features synthetic trees that bear "information rather than fruit." The thousand-foot-diameter domed structure would be connected directly to other cities by rapid transit lines.

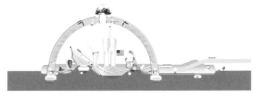

2D DENSITY RANKING	FAR RANKING	GREENSPACE RANKING	POPULATION RANKING	3D DENSITY RANKING
31/49	43/49	5/49	33/49	21/49

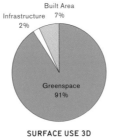

SURFACE USE 3D

Built Area 7%
Infrastructure 2%
Greenspace 91%

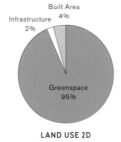

LAND USE 2D

Built Area 4%
Infrastructure 2%
Greenspace 95%

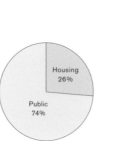

BUILT SPACE

Housing 26%
Public 74%

GREENSPACE

Wilderness 100%

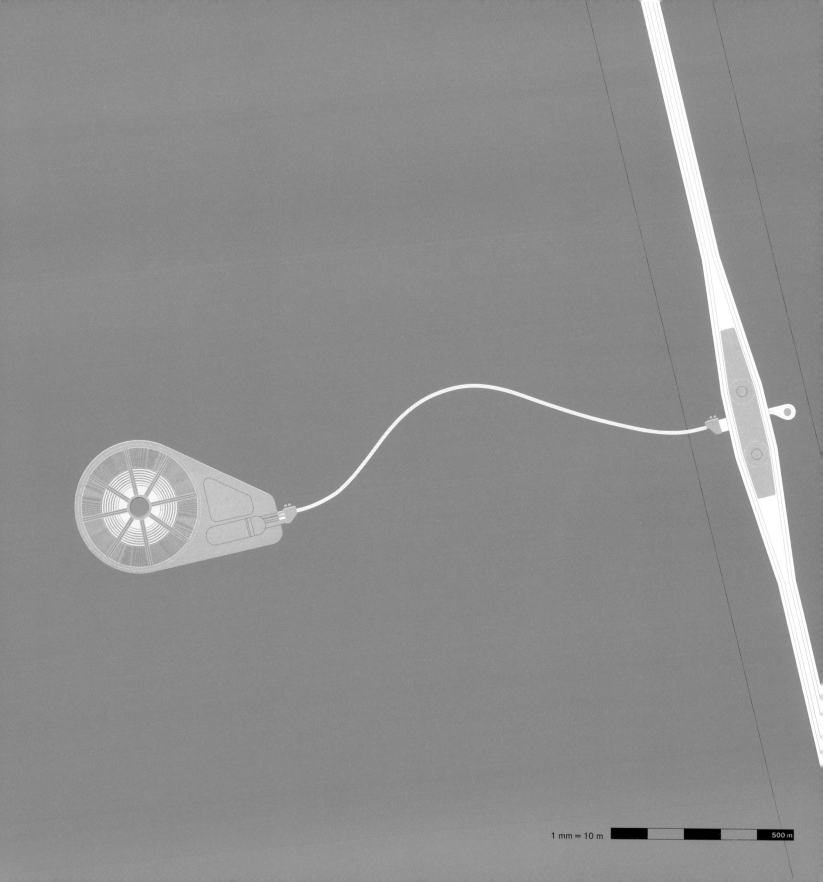

1 mm = 10 m   500 m

London, England, 1972
Rem Koolhaas

Total Site Area (2-D; in m²)	7,099,962

Total Greenspace (m²)	5,293
Area: Greenspace: agriculture	0
Area: Greenspace: lawn	0
Area: Greenspace: park	5,293
Area: Greenspace: wilderness	0

Area of Water (m²)	190,596
Area of Infrastructure (m²)	3,180,977

Total Built Area [footprint; m²)]	3,723,096
Area: Housing (footprint)	260,799
Area: Industrial (footprint)	0
Area: Public (footprint)	3,462,297

Total Population	150,000
Total number housing units	n/a
Number of people per housing unit	n/a

Total Area (3-D; in m²)	10,823,058
Number of Floors: Housing	2
Number of Floors: Industrial	1
Number of Floors: Public	2
Area: Total Built	7,446,192
Area: Housing (3-D)	521,598
Area: Industrial (3-D)	0
Area: Public (3-D)	6,924,594
Area: Open Space (Greenspace + Water + Infrastructure) (3-D)	3,376,866

FAR: 3-D Area / 2-D Area (x)	1.52

DENSITY: total population / site area (2-D) (people per km²)	21,127
DENSITY: total population / total area (3-D) (people per km²)	13,859

2-D Percentages		
Greenspace		0%
Agriculture	0%	
Lawn	0%	
Park	0%	
Wilderness	0%	
Water		3%
Infrastructure		45%
Built Area		52%
Housing	4%	
Industrial	0%	
Public	48%	
Total % of land use (can exceed 100%)		100%

3-D Percentages		
Greenspace		0%
Agriculture	0%	
Lawn	0%	
Park	0%	
Wilderness	0%	
Water		2%
Infrastructure		29%
Built Area		69%
Housing	5%	
Industrial	0%	
Public	64%	
Total % of land use		100%

The Exodus project by Rem Koolhaas, Madelon Vriesendorp, Elia Zenghelis, and Zoe Zenghelis proposes an extreme urban intervention in central London. The multifunctional monumental building features walls that separate the old city outside from the new within. The city is thus divided into "good" and "bad" halves, with a wall built around the good half. The good portion of the city becomes a zone of architectural and social perfections. Among other functions, the monumental strip includes "the tip," a front-line for architectural warfare; a ceremonial square; a park of air, fire, water, and earth; a university and scientific research complex; and a preserved portion of the existing city.

2D DENSITY RANKING	FAR RANKING	GREENSPACE RANKING	POPULATION RANKING	3D DENSITY RANKING
14/49	28/49	45/49	16/49	11/49

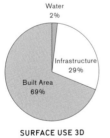

SURFACE USE 3D

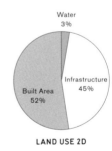

LAND USE 2D

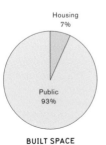

BUILT SPACE

GREENSPACE

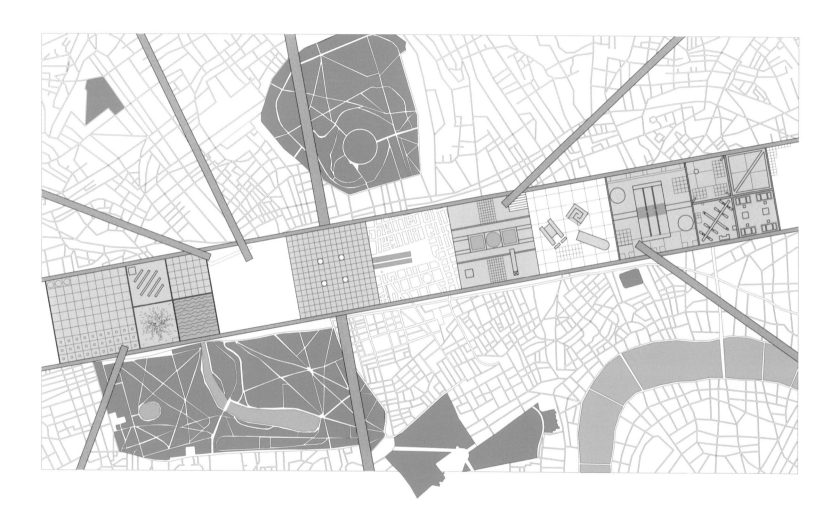

1 mm = 35 m   875 m   1750 m

Mountains, 1973
Richard Snibbe

Total Site Area (2-D; in m²)	34,367,636
Total Greenspace (m²)	**32,485,378**
Area: Greenspace: agriculture	3,401,889
Area: Greenspace: lawn	350,183
Area: Greenspace: park	4,808,958
Area: Greenspace: wilderness	23,924,348
Area of Water (m²)	**763,103**
Area of Infrastructure (m²)	**413,279**
Total Built Area [footprint; m²)]	**705,876**
Area: Housing (footprint)	291,504
Area: Industrial (footprint)	0
Area: Public (footprint)	414,372
Total Population	**60,000**
Total number housing units	20,000
Number of people per housing unit	3.00
Total Area (3-D; in m²)	**38,142,753**
Number of Floors: Housing	4
Number of Floors: Industrial	0
Number of Floors: Public	8
Area: Total Built	**4,480,992**
Area: Housing (3-D)	1,166,016
Area: Industrial (3-D)	0
Area: Public (3-D)	3,314,977
Area: Open Space (Greenspace + Water + Infrastructure) (3-D)	33,661,760
FAR: 3-D Area / 2-D Area (x)	**1.11**
DENSITY: total population / site area (2-D) (people per km²)	**1,746**
DENSITY: total population / total area (3-D) (people per km²)	**1,573**

2-D Percentages		
Greenspace		**95%**
Agriculture	10%	
Lawn	1%	
Park	14%	
Wilderness	70%	
Water		**2%**
Infrastructure		**1%**
Built Area		**2%**
Housing	1%	
Industrial	0%	
Public	1%	
Total % of land use (can exceed 100%)		**100%**

3-D Percentages		
Greenspace		**85%**
Agriculture	9%	
Lawn	1%	
Park	13%	
Wilderness	62%	
Water		**2%**
Infrastructure		**1%**
Built Area		**12%**
Housing	3%	
Industrial	0%	
Public	9%	
Total % of land use		**100%**

A proposed mountain resort complex, the Handloser project used crystal-like geometries to establish a series of settlements. The main portion of the complex was situated in a valley, and residential portions were to be in the hills above, connected to the center by a series of funiculars.

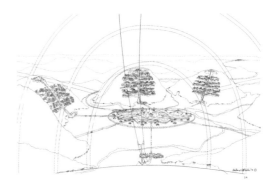

2D DENSITY RANKING	FAR RANKING	GREENSPACE RANKING	POPULATION RANKING	3D DENSITY RANKING
44/49	39/49	6/49	22/49	39/49

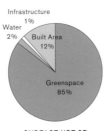

SURFACE USE 3D

Infrastructure 1%
Water 2%
Built Area 12%
Greenspace 85%

LAND USE 2D

Infrastructure 1%
Built Area 2%
Water 2%
Greenspace 95%

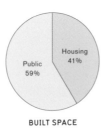

BUILT SPACE

Public 59%
Housing 41%

GREENSPACE

Agriculture 10%
Lawn 1%
Park 15%
Wilderness 74%

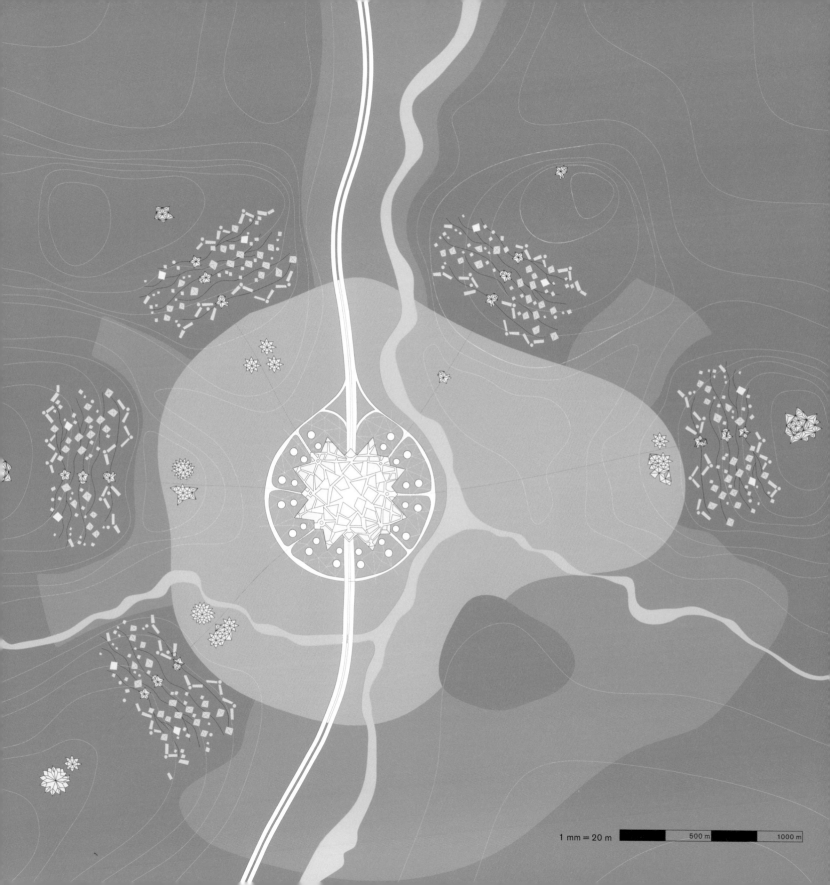

1 mm = 20 m   500 m   1000 m

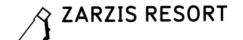

Zarzis, Tunisia, 1974
Constantino Dardi

Total Site Area (2-D; in m²)	**358,915**
Total Greenspace (m²)	**223,693**
Area: Greenspace: agriculture	
Area: Greenspace: lawn	
Area: Greenspace: park	223,693
Area: Greenspace: wilderness	
Area of Water (m²)	**-**
Area of Infrastructure (m²)	**52,476**
Total Built Area [footprint; m²)]	**91,386**
Area: Housing (footprint)	42,260
Area: Industrial (footprint)	-
Area: Public (footprint)	49,126
Total Population	**1,000**
Total number housing units	
Number of people per housing unit	
Total Area (3-D; in m²)	**761,631**
Number of Floors: Housing	8
Number of Floors: Industrial	-
Number of Floors: Public	3
Area: Total Built	**485,461**
Area: Housing (3-D)	338,084
Area: Industrial (3-D)	-
Area: Public (3-D)	147,378
Area: Open Space (Greenspace + Water + Infrastructure) (3-D)	276,169
FAR: 3-D Area / 2-D Area (x)	**2.12**
DENSITY: total population / site area (2-D) (people per km²)	**2,786**
DENSITY: total population / total area (3-D) (people per km²)	**1,313**

2-D Percentages		
Greenspace		**62%**
Agriculture	0%	
Lawn	0%	
Park	62%	
Wilderness	0%	
Water		**0%**
Infrastructure		**15%**
Built Area		**25%**
Housing	12%	
Industrial	0%	
Public	13%	
Total % of land use (can exceed 100%)		**102%**

3-D Percentages		
Greenspace		**29%**
Agriculture	0%	
Lawn	0%	
Park	29%	
Wilderness	0%	
Water		**0%**
Infrastructure		**7%**
Built Area		**64%**
Housing	44%	
Industrial	0%	
Public	20%	
Total % of land use		**100%**

Proposed at the end of the era of megastructures, the plan for Constantino Dardi's resort at Zarzis was based more on geometric experimentation than a socially utopian idea. The project features a number of purely geometric juxtapositions, but still subscribes to certain paradigms created by older megastructures, such as terraced apartments and a linear park set between two rows of housing. This obsession with geometric expression perhaps heralds the early onset of postmodernism ... and the end of visionary urbanism.

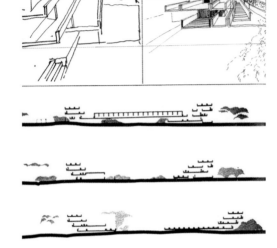

2D DENSITY RANKING	FAR RANKING	GREENSPACE RANKING	POPULATION RANKING	3D DENSITY RANKING
35/49	**19/49**	**21/49**	**47/49**	**40/49**

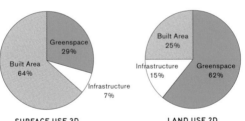

SURFACE USE 3D — Built Area 64%, Greenspace 29%, Infrastructure 7%

LAND USE 2D — Built Area 25%, Greenspace 62%, Infrastructure 15%

BUILT SPACE — Public 54%, Housing 46%

GREENSPACE — Park 100%

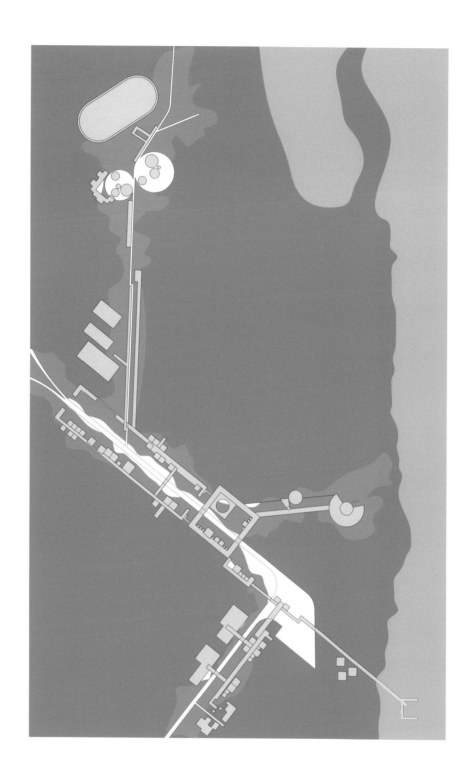

1 mm = 10 m ▮▮▮▮▮▮▮ 500 m

Total Site Area (2-D; in m²)	**6,000,000**

Total Greenspace (m²)	**2,785,652**
Area: Greenspace: agriculture	1,895,984
Area: Greenspace: lawn	0
Area: Greenspace: park	373,344
Area: Greenspace: wilderness	516,325

Area of Water (m²)	**134,241**
Area of Infrastructure (m²)	**120,106**

Total Built Area [footprint; m²)]	**2,960,000**
Area: Housing (footprint)	858,400
Area: Industrial (footprint)	562,400
Area: Public (footprint)	1,539,200

Total Population	**30,665**
Total number housing units	n/a
Number of people per housing unit	n/a

Total Area (3-D; in m²)	**9,040,000**
Number of Floors: Housing	5
Number of Floors: Industrial	5
Number of Floors: Public	5
Area: Total Built	**6,000,000**
Area: Housing (3-D)	1,740,000
Area: Industrial (3-D)	1,140,000
Area: Public (3-D)	3,120,000
Area: Open Space (Greenspace + Water + Infrastructure) (3-D)	3,040,000

FAR: 3-D Area / 2-D Area (x)	
	2.03
DENSITY: total population / site area (2-D) (people per km²)	**5,111**
DENSITY: total population / total area (3-D) (people per km²)	**3,392**

2-D Percentages		
Greenspace		**47%**
Agriculture	32%	
Lawn	0%	
Park	6%	
Wilderness	9%	
Water		**2%**
Infrastructure		**2%**
Built Area		**49%**
Housing	14%	
Industrial	9%	
Public	26%	
Total % of land use (can exceed 100%)		**100%**

3-D Percentages		
Greenspace		**31%**
Agriculture	21%	
Lawn	0%	
Park	4%	
Wilderness	6%	
Water		**1%**
Infrastructure		**1%**
Built Area		**67%**
Housing	19%	
Industrial	13%	
Public	35%	
Total % of land use		**100%**

Masdar is an (ideally) carbon-neutral, zero-waste community devised by Foster + Partners. Located on the outskirts of Abu Dhabi, it houses the headquarters for the International Renewable Energy Agency and the recently completed Masdar Institute within a walled-in, roughly gridded plan surrounded by greenhouses, research fields, and photovoltaic farms. Circulation is based entirely entirely on pedestrian traffic and public transportation, including light rail and a personal tram system. Because Masdar is currently under construction, we have updated this project's data with 2015 information provided by Foster + Partners. Subsequent development and design have increased density while decreasing site area and population, however Masdar's overall place in the standings relative to the other projects remains the same.

2D DENSITY RANKING	FAR RANKING	GREENSPACE RANKING	POPULATION RANKING	3D DENSITY RANKING
29/49	15/49	27/49	28/49	28/49

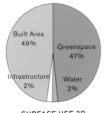

SURFACE USE 3D

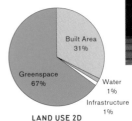

LAND USE 2D

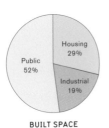

BUILT SPACE

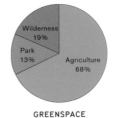

GREENSPACE

1 mm = 20 m   500 m   1000 m

ESSAYS AND COMPARATIVE DATA

SAY NOT THE STRUGGLE NAUGHT AVAILETH

A discussion with Archigram's Michael Webb, Amale Andraos, Dan Wood, and Joseph Grima

AA In Archigram's writing, the work is always set against–or in relation to–past thinking about the city or the architectural discourse of the times. I'm curious about how you positioned yourselves in reaction to what was happening around you.

MW Well, I toe the party line when it comes to that. The work we did was never about the future. It wasn't trying to predict what would happen in ten or twenty years time, but rather a reaction to what we saw around us and the innovations spreading through English society: not only technological changes (like new developments in color printing), but also the social shifts brought about by people like Mary Quant, the fashion designer, and what was happening on Kings Road and Carnaby Street. We felt that we were merely reacting to those innovations in an architectural way, which our brethren in the profession were obviously not–at least in terms of the buildings they produced.

At the same time Bucky Fuller was hugely influential on us. I quote Hugh Clough's poem "Say not the Struggle Naught Availeth," specifically the line "westward, look, the land is bright" ... In other words, we were looking to America. We got very excited about mobile homes, for example–not realizing at the time they were very far from being mobile–and drive-ins. The drive-ins! They had a huge influence on us. And yet most English architects seemed remarkably unperturbed by all these things that were happening, and were producing a rather bland version of high modernism.

DW How then did you come about to designing these enormous cities, rather than buildings?

MW In those days, it seemed almost a require-ment that everyone have a go at designing a city. That was just what one did. In the beginning, we were all working at fairly dreary day jobs, designing uninteresting buildings for uninteresting architects. We would come home from work, get together, and go all night designing cities! For about six years, we didn't take any time off.

AA We are always interested in the fact that these city projects seem to disappear

rather suddenly in the 1970s. Why do you think architects suddenly turned away from the city and the projection of big visions, after embracing them so wholeheartedly for so long?

MW Well, if you look through the Archigram opus, it starts off with Plug-in City, which is the standard megastructural city that Banham wrote about and that everyone was doing back then. There was Raimund Abraham with a city that girdled Earth, which Superstudio later took over, and so on. Then, if you take the period from '61 to '74, we moved from the megastructure as the answer to every problem to a looser, more romantic vision ... Romantic because the supporting structural/service frame tended to become hidden underground, or at least minimized, thus freeing the ground up so that a vision of the natural world might return. The drawings that David Greene did for his Living Pod or RockPlug/LogPlug look like a landscape straight out of Claude Lorraine, peopled not by Cephalus and Procris, but by somewhat hip professional types in mid-sixties dress. In Archigram's case, therefore, we started to almost miniaturize our work, ending up with little personal bubbles moving around the landscape. Then Superstudio started doing similar stuff. Hippie culture, with its seeming rejection of technology, made the megastructure city seem quaint.

DW Do you think that was also in part a reaction to the fact that giant projects–de facto megastructures–were actually getting built from the mid-'60s on? Did you suddenly realize that they weren't the urban panacea everyone had hoped for? Is that why you moved away towards more miniaturization?

MW Actually, one could say that we miniaturized ourselves out of existence! To utter a Lutheran sounding crudity, if you all may forgive me, we disappeared up our own arseholes. The question remains interesting, though: why did that happen? I think it was the miniaturization of things like telephones and the fact that you no longer needed to be in one place or have to go home to receive a telephone call. If you imagine a form of architecture capable

of changing its form and its shape, you suddenly realize you don't need the fixed building anymore: you can just go out into the wilderness and inflate something, and there you are–with all the services that heavy concrete buildings used to facilitate. That may be part of the reason for it.

I remember an article written in *Architectural Design* about the history of technology from about 1850 on. At that time, if you had a building with a steam engine in it, the steam engine would be colossal–it could occupy as much as three floors of the building within which it was housed. One could say the building was actually supporting the machinery, as opposed to the other way around. Gradually that type of machinery became miniaturized. We realized that if we miniaturized the equipment, we didn't need Plug-in City anymore.

AA While editing *49 Cities*, we had the distinct impression that Plug-in City was the closest project to the spirit of Jane Jacobs.

DW Yet whenever we paired Archigram with Jane Jacobs, everyone would laugh.

AA But then we found this Archigram quote from *Living Arts* magazine in 1963: "The recreation of environment is too often a jaded process, having to deal only with densities, allocation of space, fulfillment of regulations: the spirit of cities is lost in the process. The warning has come from William H. Whyte in *The Exploding Metropolis* and Jane Jacobs in *Death and Life of Great American Cities*. The problem facing our cities is not just that of their regeneration, but of their right to an existence." It's funny that Archigram ended up being largely associated with megastructures when in fact you were trying to describe the vitality of the city and its street life, instead of segregating it into zones and systems.

MW Right. I think you could also look at Cedric Price and see the span of his work as being on a similar track. His thinking starts with the Fun Palace and evolves towards the Potteries Thinkbelt which, by comparison, is a very modest investment; architecturally speaking– it uses old railcars and the existing rail network.

AA He's investing existing infrastructures.

MW There's a book about him by Stanley Matthews where Price talks about the Potteries Thinkbelt project. Modern telecommunications made projects like the Open University possible: a public service in which teaching happens over the radio or TV, or nowadays the Internet. In this scenario all forms of hardware are potentially redundant, and the last vestige of some tangible piece of architecture is gone. All you need is a temporary building for graduation day—and even that needs to be nothing more than a gothic set, which is where Ron Herron's Sets Project comes in. So we were all saying the same thing in our own ways, I guess.

AA Archigram always appeared to be more interested in creating environments rather than architecture: you developed ideas about what could occupy the body, connect to it, and create vitality. None of this necessarily implied a physical, built, monumental structure. Archigram uses the word environment in that quote, but with a very different meaning from our definition of environment today, which involves ecology, and by extension assumes issues of climate change and its effect on the planet. What did "environment" mean for you at the time?

MW The Cushicle project, where the building was reduced to a skin which fits around you like a bubble, was a conscious environmental statement growing out of the all too obvious over-consumption of energy implied in modern living. But it was never taken far enough to really test it out. It's all very well to show someone inside a suit rather than a building, you know, or to use phrases like "when there's no one there the building is gone" and "the building comes back to life when people return." But what does it actually mean, to think environmentally? One frequently hears statements like, "Ah, we have to have electric cars," but the real question is, as has oft been pointed out: where will the electricity to power the cars come from? Isn't the source of the electricity the equivalent of David Greene's underground supply network?

DW RockPlug and LogPlug bring up similar questions. It's a beautiful idea to plug into a log but how did the power get there?

MW Yes … one wonders what's at the other end of the cable. Like I said, we never went far enough. David never explored what happened underground, beyond the depiction of the logs. Would it be like Metropolis—an underworld of drones committed to making things pleasant for those hip professionals?

JG That evokes an image not dissimilar to postwar Britain itself, which was an incredibly stratified society. Did you see architecture as a means for intervening in this ongoing social segregation? Was there some intention of subverting the existing order?

MW I think Archigrammers were, on the surface at least, apolitical … although let us say that we were generally unconscious of, or uninterested in, the political implications of our work. Unlike Superstudio, there actually wasn't the slightest trace of activism in our work. In RockPlug, for example, David was only really interested in depicting the Elysian fields.

DW Within the world of architecture, though, you were definitely subverting status quo.

AA In researching 49 Cities, there's an interesting break that seems to happen: the early cities and utopias were always trying to find a balance or interconnection between the rural and the urban, bringing the back of house to the front. Then there is strong moment starting in the '60s, when consumerism and pop culture take over and suddenly the city becomes this completely disconnected island where you're never aware of where things come from. You use them and just toss them out, pick up a new car …

DW … cook a frozen dinner … pop a pill …

AA There's a feeling that we're all in this bubble, literally, and it's OK. This shift is so strong, it's really fascinating.

MW Recently, Dennis Crompton came to Cooper Union and showed the Archigram movie. Every time I see that movie I think, "Were we serious?" We were talking about expendability—that was one of the big words then. A fridge lasted three years, the house lasted twenty, the structure of the building lasted fifty. And then there were shots of garbage dumps with bulldozers moving old cars, airplanes, and other stuff. For those times that was perfectly OK—it was almost something to be celebrated. Had Plug-in City been implemented, the amount of garbage would have grown tenfold. Yet in the movie we didn't seem to have any problem with that at all.

JG How interested were you in actually realizing these ideas? Were they meant to remain ideas? If a developer came to you and said they had a couple of billion lying around and they were thinking of investing in Plug-in City, would you have even considered actually trying to build it?

MW It would have frightened the pants off us. The only thing that ever had a real chance of happening was the Monte Carlo project. But as soon as they figured out that the cost of the wiring alone needed to make everything would eat up the whole budget for the building, the client lost interest very quickly. It was—what is it called?—a "reality check" …
   I was talking to Dennis the other day about Peter Cook. Anyone who can accomplish what he did, start a magazine from scratch as one sheet of rather tatty paper with some vague, crudely photographed images on it, and make it into what it became, needs to have a certain type of personality. You need to be flitting around from idea to idea. So when Peter got the chance to do the Graz Museum he wisely teamed up with Colin Fournier. And of course once the project was underway and they needed to go into the next stage, persuading the city people that it should be done this way rather than that way, Peter lost interest completely, because that's his nature. But if he had the sort of personality that could see a project through, he wouldn't have started Archigram. In this world you need people like Peter, to just be irritants, and other people like the rest of us who implement the ideas. We never worried about what would get built

and what wouldn't. We were oblivious to what happened to the project once we'd made pretty drawings of it. If nothing happens that's fine; in fact, it's probably better.

AA   But later on you must have realized your influence on many projects that were built, and on many architects, like the Centre Pompidou, for example.

MW   I remember hearing they thought they had sprung out of the womb of ignorance without that much help from Archigram! In fact, I don't think they felt they owed us anything. It's obvious that we owe Fuller something, because if you look at the Montreal tower you can see misunderstood Bucky Fuller domes all over the place. They're hemispherical and suddenly they go into a funny curved shape, which Fuller would never have done.

DW   It's interesting that the Fuller influence was really almost exclusively on the surface, or in the structure. Because his drive was to achieve performance, to improve the world through science.

MW   Oh, absolutely. And God bless him for that. I don't mind representing Archigram as being arriviste, you know. Come late onto the scene and take from here and there. We probably cheered up the architectural scene in England— and maybe here as well. That's something. That makes life worthwhile.

AA   You were fresh.

MW   At the same time, if we really had studied Fuller we might have done one project every five years rather than five every year. And Wachsmann too. If you look at some of Ron's drawings, the little bit of architecture you can see in them is composed of space frame roofs à la Wachsmann. We just lifted from here and there to provide the necessary architectural backdrop.

AA   You mentioned Superstudio a few times and I would add Archizoom as well. All of you embraced the cultural moment of the time, consumption and consumerism. But you said

Archigram was apolitical while Superstudio was obviously much more critical. Archizoom was maybe somewhere in between. It seemed an interesting moment when all these groups took various positions and produced work that was not "visionary" in a Corbusian sense, but some-how more critical. And so that was one of the questions we had for *49 Cities*, where we flatten those ideological differences, were all of you in contact or very much aware of each other's work?

MW   In '71, I was at RISD and Natalini of Superstudio was there too. I got to know him very well then. It's interesting to me that the work has a commonality—it all relates. And yet, as you said, we were so apolitical and they were just the opposite—yet the work was similar. Superstudio was unable to leave its politics at home. Of course all architecture is political, whether the architect is aware of it or not, eh....?

JG   It was almost invariably the case with that generation, both there and abroad. It was exactly the same with the Metabolists. Some of them were quite left wing but they were all, almost invariably from extremely wealthy families. Were you in touch with the Metabolists at all?

MW   Not so much, at least not until later on, after the story was over, really. I do think, however, that any discussion of what we all did has to include the Futurists. Didn't they all come from rather wealthy families as well, incidentally? When I talk about the Futurists with students I have a lovely slide of a group photograph of all of them. They're not dressed like artists in velvet jackets with lilies and long hair, but like businessmen. Stiff white collars straight out of the wash, heavily starched. I remember the suppression of women was one of their gruesome aims, wasn't it? And they spoke of concepts like the "hygiene of war." Yet they also had lovely statements about racing cars and all that stuff that really inspired us.

DW   What were some of the other things that influenced your work?

MW   Well, there was an airbrush artist called L. Ashwell Wood who had a rather disproportionate

influence on my youth. I've always admired this guy's airbrush drawings and if you open a book on bridges, say, in that period, there'll be at least one beautiful airbrush job by L. Ashwell Wood. He was the best of the lot. In one book on trains he drew a cut-away cross section through Grand Central Terminal that showed everything: the subways underneath, the main concourse, the train tracks on two levels.

And at the top was a label which read "43rd Street," but located so that it appears to refer to the roof space, where there's a triangular void over the concourse. And to me, that was terribly exciting as a child, imagining that this enormous boulevard ran straight through the roof of this great train station! It inspired a lot of my thinking, in retrospect.

AA   We were recently talking with Winy Maas of MVRDV about his interview with Yona Friedman and Friedman's ideas about the Ville Spatiale. Our conversation centered around the notion of the "visionary" today. We feel that it is a time of change, of crisis and transformation, or potential transformation. And Winy suggested that we should in fact redefine the term "visionary." That it's no longer so much about the large-scale, utopian, top-down interventions, but that it's a kind of combination of idealism peppered with pragmatism. That today's visionaries should not remove themselves from the world but rather act within it. The scale of thinking is large but the scale of intervention can be quite small, or at least precise and specific, localized. Thanks to media and the way we live today, the impact can be just as great. For me, it goes back to your bubble idea. Rather than the building or the structure being enormous, through a very small intervention you can induce very large-scale consequences.

MW   I disagree, actually. As much as I love Winy, I disagree. A visionary, by definition, is a voice crying alone in the wilderness. If you pepper his idealism with pragmatism, he's no longer a visionary. God bless Soleri for his total unrealism. It's funny we didn't mention Soleri before, because there's someone who tried to build his fantasies.

Archigram's airbrushed origins: L. Ashwell Wood's
Grand Central Terminal rendering from *The World's
Railways and How They Look*, 1935

The general spirit is quite downbeat and there's a certain sense of disillusionment with the whole experiment. And from a purely pragmatic point of view, it's pretty clear his buildings are an ecological disaster, in terms of the energy that they actually consume and the embedded energy that was required to build them. Wanting to build Arcosanti was perfectly comprehensible, of course, but the aura of defeat that lingers over it now goes a long way to explain the distrust with which our generation contemplates visionary projects like Arcosanti, or even your own.

AA Yet on the other hand I think we lack the visionary today. When you abandon it entirely, when you abandon the ability to think abstractly, and to project a different way of being, there is very little left …

MW I know this is a diversion, but I'll tell you all the same—thinking about the Futurists, you know their whole manifesto starts off not with the clauses of the manifesto but describing how, as young people on a hot summer night they sat outside, surrounded by braziers of flames spiraling up into the night sky, and began talking and drinking, and having all these lovely ideas about what they were going to do with their life. It's so reminiscent of one's own youth, don't you think? Talking all night long. I was looking for a phrase I found in the Painter's Manifesto. Something like: "The bus travels through the city and it enters into the homes of the people living there." It's beautiful. The inhabitants of the city hear the bus, they think of the people inside the bus, and they in turn enter into the bus through their awareness of the bus. It's beautiful, the vehicle merging into the city and becoming a part of it and vice versa.

You know, for me this has been a really nice reexamination of what I was up to and what everyone else was up to and where it all layered together.

AA His first small project, Cosanti, in Scottsdale, is really beautiful.

MW To me, somehow, none of his built work captures the feel of his drawings though. There were two giant drawings he had in a show in '79 at the Drawing Center. I think the show was called *Visionary Drawings: Architecture and Planning*. Soleri had drawn these incredible monster skyscrapers. Beautiful. He had this idea that there would be tubes and ducts running around the skin, and cool air would be blue and warm air red, just like it shows whether a human being is feeling warm or cold. The buildings would change color according to whether it was warm air blowing through or cold air. Somehow Arcosanti has become this sort of Aztec reminiscence. It didn't achieve the transition from visionary image to built reality, but that's

also another conversation. I think Raimund Abraham also found it difficult to transform the drawn image into built image. Natalini, on the other hand, is in the opposite camp. He gave up all that square grid stuff as soon as he started building.

AA Except for the furniture.

DW The thing is, if you cover the globe with a grid, it actually has to curve …

MW Damn it, you're right!

JG In a way Soleri's work is a really apt example. I visited Arcosanti and Cosanti last winter, and there's an unmistakable despondency in the crumbling beauty of the place. Not just the architecture—even the people who live there.

Michael Webb is a founding member of the influential Archigram Group. Since 1965 Webb has lived in the US and taught architecture at The Cooper Union, Columbia University, and a number of other schools.

RESURRECTING THE DODO: THE DEATH AND LIFE OF URBAN PLANNING

Sam Jacob

Sitting in the Burger King in the center of Almere—the Dutch new town built on land reclaimed from the North Sea—it suddenly struck me that this might be the culmination of the entire history of urbanism. Chewing on a Bacon Double Swiss, I looked out of the burger joint onto the neighboring multiplex, the empty public square, the parking garage, the shops that lead up to the station and out towards the houses, where tree-lined roads lead out to fields where expanses of sand are marked with colored flags ready for foundations for new estates to be laid. This whole landscape has been transformed from seabed, dredged up into city and given form and structure by the imaginative force of urban planning.

Almere is a synthetic city that forms the full stop at the end of the end of the history of urban planning. Its direct conceptual heritage springs from post-WWII new towns built in an era of optimism that allied a technocratic, top-down form of planning with a belief in social democracy. It and they are laced with DNA from visionary high modernist plans such as the Ville Radieuse, which in turn fall under the influence of the Garden Cities of Ebenezer Howard. Almere, whose first house was completed in 1976, might be the only surviving relative of this family tree—the last dodo in a lineage of urban planning stretching back like a biblical dynasty in which x begat y and y begat z and z begat … and so on back through time. Soon after Almere's founding, however, the entire conception of urban planning changed.

At the end of the twentieth century, the idea of urban design as a method of making the world a better place collapsed. Firstly, it came under a sustained attack from unholy alliances from both left and right, from radicals and royalty. An orgy of strange bedfellows whose cast included Jane Jacobs and Prince Charles, New Urbanists and anarchists and so on who added their voices to an atonal chorus attacking the principles of top-down Modernist planning. These multiple and contradictory agendas formed not a coherent argument but an unanswerable force that cracked the structure of the discipline. Guilt and failure took the place of utopian positivism. The ideologies, methodologies, internal momentum, and ambitions that had sustained

a hundred years of progressive planning suddenly evaporated.

Disciplinary crisis is one thing (and not necessarily a bad thing). But the real change in urban planning wasn't precipitated by public debate, by arguments around the role or nature of urban planning. It was a shift in the conditions of planning itself. Urban planning as a public project conceived and implemented by government intended for the public good vanished. It became a project undertaken by private enterprise whose motivation remains first and foremost profit. From the '80s onwards, the bodies that undertook planning became those of deregulated government. Private and quango-ized public/private institutions became the mechanisms of planning and development. And under these conditions, the entire conception of planning changed.

At its core, the modernist project could be characterized by the desire to emancipate. This was the moo of twentieth-century urban planning, the thing which animated its actions. In the Reaganite/Thatcherite landscape and beyond, cities would no longer be conceived as mechanisms of social democracy, but solely as instruments of the market. We should regard the dismantling of this moo as a highly politicized act of ideology.

The famous photograph of Le Corbusier's hand, disembodied, hovering over a model of the Ville Radieuse is an image that encapsulates a particular power relationship between the creator and the city, setting the architect as a powerful visionary forming the city's physical shape. The hand reached down from above, creating a city and a society in the manner of a sculptor shaping clay.

In our deregulated, neoliberal context, there is another kind of hand looming over us. But it's not the hand of a visionary designer, nor the hand of an explicit ideology. It is the 'invisible hand' of Adam Smith, the hand of the market. This hand shapes our landscapes through its own kind of mojo: self-interest, competition, supply, and demand.

Modernist planning was characterized by a totalized approach that seamlessly combined a vision of society with the means by which it might be manifested. Neoliberal,

free market urban planning is a much more diffuse, slippery entity. This might explain characteristics of architecture and urban planning projects of the last decades. In the absence of a modernist mojo we see heightened formalism—as though form has ballooned to fill the space vacated by ideology.

In place of ideology comes lifestyle, most obviously articulated in Richard Florida's *The Rise of the Creative Class*. Florida imagines a demographic, termed "the creative class," composed of high-tech workers, artists, musicians, lesbians, and gay men. He argues that high concentrations of these "high bohemians" "correlate with a higher level of economic development and form an open, dynamic, personal and professional urban environment." Thus prosperity (neoliberalism's reinvention of emancipation) is not a function of the physicality of traditional urban planning—infrastructure and so on—but is created out of hip-ville gentrification. Urban planning's mojo is reinvented as a form of diffuse hype or vague vibe that somehow remakes our cities. Architects are part of Florida's "solution"—not because of their professionalism, or their intellectual or design ability, but because of their membership of the creative class: their taste in music, the way they dress, and where they hang out. Florida remakes the sensation of Modernism's totalized vision of the city. Except here the conceptual glue is not emancipation, but a high bohemian lifestyle.

Under the conditions of neoliberal urban planning, we can no longer engage in Modernism's utopian program of social emancipation. But that doesn't mean we don't want to make a better world. We might argue that this desire for good-doing has been replaced with environmental concern as a means by which architects and planners might address the public good. The Green agenda argues that by understanding the environmental impact of architecture and the city and then developing energy-efficient and environmentally responsible ways of building we not only address issues of resources and climate change but also fulfill sentiments that we expect architecture (or architects) to exhibit.

Our current approach to sustainability, however, is characterized as a technological issue that can be "solved" through engineering. And—like engineering—sustainability as an idea in urban planning presents itself as ideologically transparent. In other words, it does not declare a position beyond its technical remit. In this, it echoes neoliberalism's apparent ideological disengagement. But it's this appearance of benign practicality that makes neo-liberalism lethal, like a colorless, odorless anesthetizing gas. Equally, sustainability used as a justification for architecture and urban planning is disingenuous. Even if projects lived up to their zero carbon billing (without recourse to smudging the books by offsetting) their only achievement would be not making the world any worse. By isolating sustainability as a purely technical issue, it becomes a degraded echo of Modernism's totalizing ambition that synthesized the technological with social and political ideologies.

These are just a number of characteristics of mojo-less urban design. On the one hand it is politically and ideologically disengaged. On the other, it must be fragmented so that the relationship between cause and effect—or rather what it does and why it does it—are divorced. We might well wonder if there is anything urban designers can do except illustrate neoliberal Floridian visions of hipville urbanism with a small carbon footprint?

The pressing concern is how we might respond to the terms under which contemporary urban planning is carried out. How might we make sense and develop tactics that resurrect a relevant and progressive practice? The first point of resistance to neoliberalism might well be history—a way to counter its end-of-history philosophy. If neoliberalism argues that we occupy a post-historical moment and a post-ideological condition, then collapsing the entire weight of history into our present circumstance might form the basis of escape. Not history in its received form but reevaluated and cut loose from its usual theoretical and artistic significance. This brewing cocktail of utopias, ideologies, solutions, and tactics could suggest hybrid trajectories that might help us evade the fate neoliberalism delivers us up to.

Such a practical yet culturally rich toolkit might help in reformulating and reanimating the discipline of planning and at the same time

inform detailed decisions in design work. What, for example, if the figures suggested by Paolo Soleri's Mesa City coincidently chimed with planning policy in Milton Keynes and thus began to suggest the most unlikely of hybrids? Could you fuse disparate elements together to create, for example, floating, linear, garden-Ville Radieuse's? Might the non-judgemental re-assessment of these projects allow us to recompose the languages of urban planning outside of the traditional partisan arguments? And in doing this might we forge solutions that address present concerns that learn from histories real and fictional, ancient, and modern?

Sam Jacob is principal of Sam Jacob Studio and previously was a founding director of FAT Architecture. Jacob is Professor of Architecture at the University of Illinois at Chicago, visiting professor at Yale School of Architecture, and Director of Night School at the Architectural Association.

HIPPIES WITH LAB COATS

A discussion between Ant Farm's Chip Lord and Curtis Schreier, Dan Wood, and Amale Andraos

INTRODUCTION

CHIP LORD   The three main partners in Ant Farm—myself, Curtis Schreier, and Doug Michels—all had architecture degrees, but we were also entrenched in the counterculture. We were hippies. We had pretty much rejected the traditional practice of architecture, but we were still interested in the idea of designing communities. We did quite a few projects before Convention City that dealt with ideas of community and networks.

The Truckstop Network Project, for example, was an early idea for a utopian community based on a group of people who would be constantly moving around the United States in customized vehicles. We tried to create a self-contained package to travel around with: the Media Van and a trailer that we pulled behind it. It was called the Media Van because we had a portable video camera: the Sony Portapak, which in 1970 was a new product. We just had the one camera and recorder but we could use the van to play back and edit video along the way. The vehicles would be transportable, temporary, and modular. They would include a big inflatable that could be reconfigured.

We envisioned a nationwide network. At each of these truck stops would be a community center, which take the form of a simulated main street and would provide access to services, including things like video access, laser access, and computer information.

This was in 1971, long before the Internet. We imagined that when you pulled into a truck stop you could have a video call to any of the other nodes on the network, providing a way of keeping in communication with other people who were in this completely nomadic community.

We had no technical background for knowing how to create a network, no idea at that time how to give people access to computers or what exactly they would do with them, but we knew that technology should be part of this idea of a community along with more prosaic aspects, such as a daycare center and access to medical services. You can see that the design is influenced by Archigram and 1960s ideas about off-the-shelf, component-based architecture that could be plugged together. Another influence was the NASA space program. The first lunar landing was in 1969, and the idea of a completely

self-contained environment was fascinating for a lot of architects.

Of course we never went past this stage of imagining what the community might be. What we did do was just go out and model the idea ourselves with the Media Van.

We did a series of demonstrations of the package at college campuses. We would inflate the inflatables: a solar heated shower, ICE 9, a tent to sleep in, and a kitchen that were all built into this trailer. That lasted a few months. The other thing we were doing was meeting people we had connected with, primarily through the mail—a network of people who were working with this portable video equipment. It was considered to be amateur quality, yet there was a movement that realized it was a form of alternative television programming: that cameras, in the hands of average people, could make works that were shot at "ground level," rather than the overview of the network news.

What's interesting about the Media Van project is the modesty of the reality versus the intended scale: the utopian idea of a nationwide network.

In 1972, after the Truck Stop Tour, the Media Van was repainted and reconfigured for the group Top Value Television (TVTV) for a project that brought together an ad-hoc group of video artists and others to go to the political conventions in Miami Beach and make alternative video coverage.

That year, both the Republican and Democratic conventions were in the same city. There was an incumbent president, Richard M. Nixon, who had inherited the Vietnam War. The candidate the Democrats put forward was known as a peace candidate, George McGovern. At the Republican Convention there were a lot of protestors, including a group known as the Vietnam Veterans Against the War, led by Ron Kovic, a paralyzed veteran who had written *Born on the Fourth of July*. We went to Miami in the media van, and while we were there we found a roll of film that some young Republican had lost. Apparently he had gone out to the airport to greet President Nixon and his wife and then attended the convention. We used these images in a series of collage projects. One showed Nixon speaking on the third night of the convention after the nomination.

There's an image from the convention, showing Doug Michels of Ant Farm, who was one of the TVTV videographers, back to back with a CBS cameraman. Doug has the Sony Portapak, in contrast to the network's big reel-to-reel camera. The funny thing about this picture is that Doug is wearing these purple bell-bottoms, and the CBS cameraman is wearing striped bell-bottoms!

One of the accomplishments of the project by TVTV was that the barrier to broadcasting— the half-inch tape—was broken, and it became possible to broadcast an alternative of what was happening, what was being orchestrated by the parties and the convention.

CONVENTION CITY (CHIP LORD AND CURTIS SCHREIER)

After the conventions, in the fall of 1972, Ant Farm went out to Houston, where we were living, and proposed a workshop with students at Rice University, to design a Convention City that would be self-contained and would have the flexibility

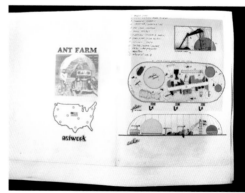

Truckstop Network, Doug Michels, 1970.

to house different types of conventions, and that would also be the world's largest television studio! The idea was that it would be both a permanent city and a temporary city of hotel rooms where people would come to the convention.

CURTIS SCHREIER What people don't realize was the dome that we showed surrounding the city was actually the hotel rooms themselves. It shows in the section, but not very well in the model. The 20,000 delegates were in the hotel rooms, and they were the citizens of the city.

CL They'd have a balcony to look down from the dome to the floor of the convention, which we made into this psychedelic landscape. It's a very dichromatic model. You can gauge the scale of the project from the Boeing 747 we included in the renderings.

CS There were state-shaped platforms for the delegates where everyone would stand. One person, representing the people behind them, would work their way to the front of the delegation and that person got to go down the escalator and stand and vote on the issue. The voting floor was supposed to be a sensitive floor.

CL An illuminative, responsive, programmable floor.

CS The delegates would ride on little electric bumper cars. That was the voting process. You would have collisions with others with different ideas, and be able to push people into certain corners.

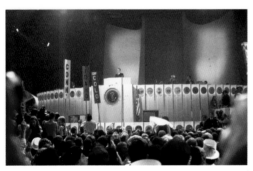
Republican National Convention, Miami Beach, Florida, 1972.

CL This is at the core of the idea. The conventions are already like game shows; they build very temporary sets just to be seen on camera. Convention City presented an optimized platform for a new way of voting. We also thought it would be interactive with people at home, who could talk back to their TV. Maybe they could have input remotely.

CS In Convention City, the public was also able to see what was going on, on the floor, from a people-mover that had viewing areas as it swirled around the top of the dome. There would be a certain amount of interaction with the delegates, there might be common lounges. There'd be a lot of history. Partly world's fair and partly bicentennial celebration. The space program was really big. We called the lake Mercury Lake after the astronauts. We were going to actually make it so it looked like it was silver. We couldn't use real mercury, but that would have been cool. It was a celebration. There's also a section that looks like a giant tree trunk that was supposed to trace all the roots of American ancestry out as an exhibition. There were all kinds of things that were designed.

CL It was a one-week workshop, and during that time the model was made as well as all the drawings. At the end of the workshop, we put the model on a stand covered in American flag bunting and held a press conference.

CS It was part of the performance to surround the model with the red, white, and blue bunting. We presented to the press as if it were an Americana thing, rather than a high art thing.

CL: This was one of Doug Michel's great abilities as a publicist. It was a matter of writing a press release and sending it out to every TV station and newspaper. It gives you an insight into how things like that turn up as news items. So, it was a crazy idea in one sense, but then it was taken seriously because it was written up in the press. The paper wrote it up as, "these guys are ready to go to the next stage of design as soon as they find a developer." And you know, in Houston, Texas, a developer might well have come forward! We needed the newspaper for that and we had

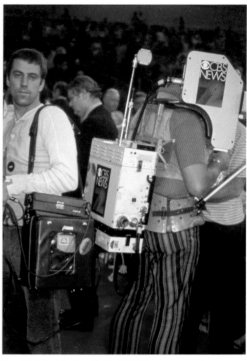
Doug Michels of Ant Farm (left) with CBS cameraman at the Republican National Convention, Miami Beach, Florida, 1972.

some calls I think, but the ideal developer and the ideal site were not to be found.

DISCUSSION (DAN WOOD, AMALE ANDRAOS, CHIP LORD)

DW I love the contradictions in the project, which really stem very directly from your experiences at the conventions in 1972, and the idea of the political convention in general. On the one hand you have this very temporary, Potempkin-esque situation of something constructed very cheaply and quickly. On the other hand, through graphics and symbolism a very strong image of power and the political process is created. That's why your final presentation of the project with the bunting is so great, it transforms the project into something very American and something truly political.

AA I was thinking of how you started your presentation by describing the modesty of interventions versus the scale of the ideas. This can be very strategic. A stealthy network of small nodes can produce big changes. But you still go for the big scale: this amazing landscape under an enormous bubble of hotel rooms. And in the end, with the press conference and the bunting, there's still this visible, strategic intervention added. How do you see the two together?

CL   Well, if you contrast Convention City with the Truckstop Network, for example, one is completely conceptual and the other one is completely practical. For Ant Farm at the time, the two approaches don't necessarily ever come together, they're really different. I think today the question is really how do you make architecture for the virtual, or in the virtual? I don't know the answer. At the same time we have more capability to build large places and large spaces. It's probably important to try and consider how to integrate large public spaces with handheld capabilities to enhance a sense of social democracy. That seems kind of obvious but it's still good to state it.

AA   The fact is that, with the Arab Spring for example, we can see that with all the organizing done through social media, people still needed to consolidate in a public, physical space like Tahir Square. The virtual still hasn't replaced the physical; they compliment each other. That's why Convention City is so interesting, and so visionary. It illustrates this notion that in the end the physical has not been entirely displaced, but can be complimented or enhanced through interactivity and media. It is interesting to compare Convention City with Fuller's Dome over Manhattan project, which encloses the urban to somehow make it more of a self-sustaining system. Convention City, on the other hand, encloses this amazing representation of landscape. Do you have sense as to why you felt that the idea of a landscape was so important to the project?

CL   I think it was a form of expressionism really. An expressive sculptural landscape seemed to best represent the sense of multiple permutations of what could happen, to emphasize it was a transformable and active space.

AA   The other thing that's interesting is the site plan drawing of Convention City. In contrast with many of the other projects in 49 Cities, Convention City is shown plugging into something with a kind of umbilical cord.

DW   There's the city, the plug, and the idea that there's the rest of the world beyond, which you have to leave and enter into this new world, while still remaining connected.

CL   It's connected to a highway, a core that accommodates both physical mobility and telecommunications capability. That's why it can be positioned anywhere in the world. The idea that you can ignore what's around you, the environment, is obsolete. You can't really do that unless you make it a capsule that's also completely off-grid and self-sufficient and so on.

AA   We also asked this question in our conversation with Michael Webb. He admitted that at the time, the context and environment weren't ever present in their cities, it was the Pop appeal of disposability. So even though it was called the Plug-in City," the plug was never shown.

CL   Right. Plugged into what?

AA   Exactly. It simply wasn't a concern. I think that there's a shift in your work, just in that drawing it's very clear that you're never unplugged, or if you are, you have to think about how you could be.

AA   I think this also relates to this notion of the disposable convention, the creation of a stage set that gets thrown away.

CL   These conventions are like instant cities. It might be thirty or forty thousand people coming and inhabiting this area for a short period of time and then leaving.

DW   When we talked to Michael Webb, we were asking "Why cities?" He said simply that everyone was doing it! You had to have your city. I was wondering whether part of that was that Ant Farm had done so much and at some point you thought, We have to do a city as well!

CL   It really came out of the experience of going to the convention in 1972. It was a simple leap to turn it into this project, to bring it back to architecture. Also, "Convention City" is a good name. The idea was essentially putting everybody in one big dome and having no cars. That was the organizing principle. It doesn't necessarily take on the full

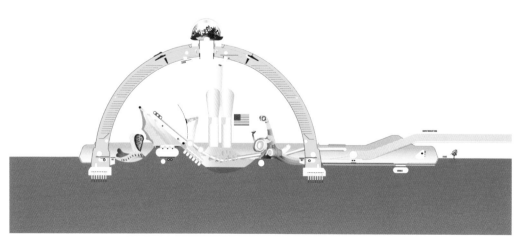

Convention City, Ant Farm, 1972. Drawing by WORKac, 2015.

responsibility of what it means to these twenty thousand people. I suppose everybody who lived there would be working in the service industry of the convention. Is that the kind of city you want to live in? We didn't answer those questions.

DW   I wanted to talk about the idea of the project as satire. I think Convention City can definitely be read as political commentary, and I think probably a lot of people do. But I get the feeling that Ant Farm did not.

CL   It's maybe not the most overt presentation of satire, or irony, but isn't the concept and the title a form of political commentary? Of course there was a sense of satire simply by the idea of the world's largest TV studio. But we took that initial gesture and created this city with more than one energy, as we were saying. So would that be satire?

DW   You have described Ant Farm as hippies with lab coats. I think it is funny that in that picture of Doug Michels it's very hard to tell which one is the hippie and which is the CBS cameraman. I know the idea of the counter culture was very important to you. Did you always feel that the counter culture could eventually become the culture and therefore truck stops and

the Internet would become less radical, but very real, versions of your proposals?

CL   I think the central tension of our practice was whether a true alternative culture could be created. That was a larger project, the larger goal, and we were just the architects. We have different forms of realization. Tom Hayden, who was a radical who became a politician; radical food people of that era have became restaurateurs. But can there be such a thing as a true alternative culture? To create something that's truly an alternative is very challenging. It has to, at some point interface with the existing culture. Within Ant Farm there was a kind of "bad boy" aspect—just do things that would make an impact or send a message as an affront to mainstream culture. But at any moment a potential real client might show up and we always felt maybe we can make it work with this client, because they are actually interested in funding the ideas.

DW   It is something that always comes up when talking about *49 Cities*: to what degree were these proposals meant to be realized? For us, in the end, it does not really matter. These are ideas that have helped shape reality, and vice versa. Paper architecture can sometimes have a bigger impact on the broader culture than built architecture.

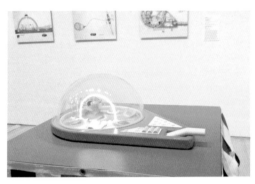

Photo of the Convention City model in the exhibition *The Utopian Impulse: Buckminster Fuller and the Bay Area*, 2012, San Francisco Museum of Modern Art.

CL   We were of course influenced by Archigram. We wanted to be part of this underground culture that was opposed to the mainstream culture. There were underground newspapers and underground radio, underground art. An Ant Farm is "underground architecture"—a very literal metaphor. It was also a good metaphor for what we were engaged in because the ants work collaboratively and the shapes they make underground are pretty amazing. We didn't know this in 1968, but there's been more recent scientific research into ant colonies. It describes a collective mind, a collective intelligence the ants have. There are billions of ants in the world. It's a species that's very adaptable, very enduring in terms of their habitats. They also make amazing architecture above ground too, huge structures. This idea that the colony has a greater mind than the individual ant is pretty interesting, all of the individual actions function for the good of the colony. Ant Farm was a collective—a team, with a kind of collective mind. At a larger scale, I always felt that by acting as visionary architects, we might be part of an even larger intelligence, the collective cultural intelligence.

Chip Lord and Curtis Schreier are co-founders, with Doug Michels (1943-2003), of Ant Farm—a radical art and architecture collective. They both live in San Francisco and Lord is a Professor Emeritus in the Film & Digital Media Department at UC Santa Cruz. Lord and Schreier continue to collaborate, most recently with WORKac for the 2015 Chicago Biennial.

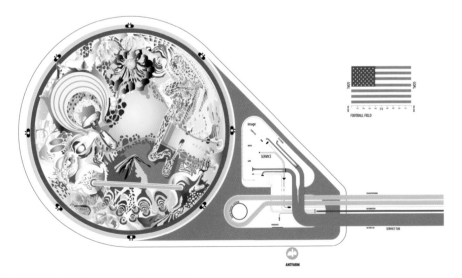

Convention City, Ant Farm, 1972. Drawing by WORKac, 2015.

EVERYTHING INTERCONNECTED

A correspondence between
Yona Friedman and Dan Wood

Dear Dan Wood,

I send you here short answers to your questions. A preliminary remark: I consider everything interconnected. Separating topics might lead to misunderstanding.

Could you describe briefly the Bridge-Town over the Channel project of 1963 and its origins? Was it in response to a sense that a bridge would allow for a new kind of inhabitation and exploitation that a channel tunnel never could?
The Bridge-Town over the Channel shows the way to use "Ville Spatiale" techniques for interconnecting geographic areas. Such a project could trigger large scale socioeconomic reorganization. The project was conceived without reference to the mainstream bridge or tunnel projects.

One important aspect of the Ville Spatiale is its relationship with the cities below it and the hinterland that is liberated by the city's densification, yet in the Bridge-Town Over the Channel project its isolation over water creates a very different relationship.
The "Ville Spatiale," like all cities, endeavors to be a microcosm, producing its own livelihood. At the 1975 UN conference on habitat, I suggested a program: "Habitat means food and roof."

We were always curious as to whether you intended the project as a continuous city running between England and the continent, or rather as a more isolated city set somewhere along the bridge's length?
The channel bridge I proposed as a hub: a crossing of sea traffic and land traffic, with vertical exchange—a new kind of harbor.

Was there any thought to the relationship between the Bridge-Town and the resources needed to sustain its population? Was it intended as more of an industrial city than a true metropolis with a more diverse mix of uses?
For a city, it is not the planner's intention that counts. What determines the city is the everyday behavior of the inhabitants. A slow process …

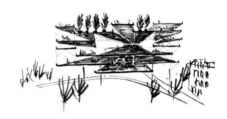

Farming Bridge, Yona Friedman, 1962.

We have seen a sketch from 1962 for a "farming bridge." Did you pursue this idea of agricultural production in other projects? Would farming in the space frame have been part of life in a Ville Spatiale?
Habitat equals food and roof.

Was the linear form unique to the later bridge town proposals (Gibraltar, Tel Aviv, Huangpu, Marseille, etc.) or do you feel that the linear arrangement could have been common to all of the Villes Spatiales? Many of your sketches incorporate road or transport infrastructure below, and it seems that a linear arrangement could have been the most economical configuration.
Linear disposal comes from local context. For me, function can fit form.

Who was part of the GEAM group and how long was the group in existence?
I presented my idea on "mobile architecture" at Ciamx in 1956. Younger participant adhered: Aujame, Kühne, Soltan. Later, in 1957: Trapman, Otto, and Günschel (after Kühne published my first paper on the topic). In 1958 I finished my manifesto on the topic, and invited a few friends to form the GEAM. Later, many young people joined. I asked all members to come up with their ideas. Ideas being exhausted, the group dissolved itself in 1962.

Why do you think it was so important for visionary architects to design entire cities in the 1960s and '70s, and why do you think this is no longer the case? With increasing population, increasing urbanization and the dangers of climate change, it does seem important to think about the city and especially the relationship between cities?
Architects' game is to imagine a city, emphasizing several factors. My motivation came through the early discovery that the central person is the user and not the planner: hardware should be transformable continuously. Contrarily to what I was taught as a student, I discovered that the average man does not exist … One last note: I don't believe in utopias, but in reality. I don't believe in planning, but in improvisation. Presently I try to launch "architecture without building." Improvisation in architecture is possible. In these last years I had to occasion to materialize test cases: giving technical instructions (my role) leaving local people to improvise on the site (without blueprints).

With all the best,
Yona

Dear Yona,

I enjoyed reading your short answers to my questions; they were very enlightening. I am also very glad that you have now received our book *49 Cities.*

While our book does certainly embrace the idea that architects and planners should be taken more seriously in their proposals for visionary cities—and that even the most far-flung ideas could have some practical implications for the design of cities—I think that what was most important for us was simply to re-inject the idea that architects and planners should be involved in large-scale thinking.

I am thinking about this in relation to your ideas regarding improvisation and the centrality of the user, which run throughout all of your work. One could argue, I suppose, that this conception runs completely counter to the aims of a book like *49 Cities,* which looks at the very physical propositions of the plans in order to determine their performance, and in a way ignores the individuals, the unplanned and the informal.

However, one of the great discoveries, in a way, of *49 Cities* for us was the importance that infrastructure plays in many of the examples in the book. Hausmann's Boulevards in Paris,

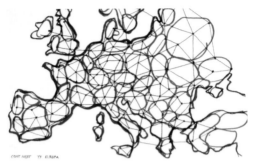

Continent City, Yona Friedman, 1959.

for example, can be read in many ways, but it can perhaps be most successfully argued as a form of infrastructure: those boulevards allowed Paris to install plumbing and subways and to transform itself from a medieval city into a modern city.

I think therefore what sets your ideas about the city apart from others who emphasize community-based planning is exactly this idea of an infrastructure. Of course the space-frame of the Villes Spatiales is perhaps the most visually dramatic. It seems to me that the infrastructure provides not only the guide or framework, but also the vision. And that while understandably you do not believe in utopias, this idea of "vision: remains critically important if a goal is truly "large scale socio-economic reorganization."

I would be interested in your ideas about infrastructure, and how these ideas may have evolved over time. While the role of infrastructure is very clear in many of your proposals, I am also interested that you mention working "without blueprints" at the end of your note—are you currently moving even further from the idea of providing an infrastructure of any sort?

I am also interested whether at any moment you investigated in more detail the role of infrastructure for the Villes Spatiales—and specifically how perhaps the space-frame would provide not only a structural infrastructure, but perhaps also deal with waste, energy, water, transport etc. Also were "food" and "roof" always imagined as separate spheres? (ie "food" on the ground,

and "roof" overhead) or were these sometimes combined or transposed?

Also if you would like to comment on the idea of "vision" and the importance of perhaps a singular voice in giving, for example "technical instructions" or setting the scene for the slow process of transformation, and whether you feel that this is a skill that architects and planners have—or should have?

Warmest regards,
Dan

Dear Dan,

Thanks for your letter and for the book. I really like it, and the approach it presented.

I personally try to avoid large scale planning except the case of my project Metropole Europe: A Continent City, based on the existing fast train network (TGV), a project I tried to defend from 1959 on (the channel bridge is a part of the project). It is more a guideline idea than a technical project: in the meantime, it tends towards realization, by itself, in a way.

This idea is an example of why I feel suspicious about planning: it is social behavior that made possible that reality (and infrastructure, you would say—but in this case the infrastructure, the railway network, dates from the mid-nineteenth century.) It became very different from its initial concept …

I think we live in a period of overplanning and overbuilding. The negative secondary effects start to pop up …

My idea about planning is that is should be as "elastic" as possible, to be adaptable to unexpected reality. Human behavior is quite unpredictable, but it is that behavior that makes a plan work. Politicians know it well, even if they try to circumvent it.

According to that idea, I think it is necessary to conceive urban infrastructure as changeable as possible. In my idea about the "Ville Spatiale" I was careful to reduce the structure's impact at ground level to a minimum: an impact point at about every 100 to 150 meters. This makes possible easy changes at the road network, sanitation, etc., without the demolitions etc., imposed by present mainsteam urban hardware.

This thought raises the problem of "urban proximity" under a new light.

"Proximity" was, during history, the master idea of city planning: defense and security up to the nineteenth century, economic factors (infrastructure costs, commercial rentability, even urban culture) till the present day.

But, psychology and technology are brutally changing. Batteries can replace network electricity, rainwater capture can provide water, phones are no more network bound, sewage disposal can be individual. Physical networks, except for commuting, are not necessarily indispensable.

And commuting? People in most jobs (about eighty percent) can (and do) work through immaterial networks. Sales and buying goes through the web, cultural exchange also. The modern city can function with a largely immaterial infrastructure: this is today's reality.

People changed, also their style of life, too. A few years ago, I wrote a booklet (or, rather, a "slide show") on "architecture without building." We don't need anymore a large part of our premises, we can operate nearly everything from home, or from anywhere, having our iPads with us …

Another new factor, emerging in cities is what I called (in 1958) "urban agriculture": kitchen gardens inserted into many-floored buildings.

Future city is open to improvisation: the "Villa Spatiale" has no definite floorpans, nor fixed facades. In 1970, my project for the Pompidou Center had no facade, it had twenty different facades—the building could change its shape for every new exhibition … it was not understood at that time.

I think we might rediscover "urban improvisation" (I write rediscover because it existed already in many civilizations).

It is a long letter as I tried to present ideas which might seem unfamiliar.

With warmest regards,
Yona

Yona Friedman is a Hungarian-born French architect, urban planner, and designer. Friedman developed the idea of a city suspended within a space frame, the Ville Spatiale, while continually inventing new ways for people to live.

	Year Built	Total Average Ranking	Pop Density (2D)	Total Pop	% Greenspace	FAR	Density by Land Use (3D)
Radiant City	1935	1	17	5	1	17	15
Tetrahedral City	1965	2	2	9	23	1	23
Dome over Manhattan	1960	3	1	10	40	7	1
Plug-in City	1964	4	6	14	30	12	3
Fort Worth	1956	5	4	17	31	8	6
Continuous Monument	1969	6	7	8	34	14	5
No-Stop City	1969	7	8	34	8	20	7
Latin American City	1650	8	12	15	18	24	12
Communitas 1	1947	9	16	2	11	42	11
Roman City	-50	10	10	25	20	25	9
Hauptstadt	1958	11	11	16	25	29	10
Frankfurt	1963	12	3	36	42	9	2
Paris (1850)	1850	13	19	7	35	11	20
Noahbabel Arcology	1969	14	13	21	41	6	18
Le Mirail	1962	15	18	26	22	22	14
Linear City	1967	16	14	24	39	10	16
Fun Palace	1965	17	5	41	47	4	8
Mesa City	1960	18	37	6	9	5	48
New Babylon	1960	19	9	12	46	35	4
Masdar City	2006	20	29	19	28	15	26
Helix City	1961	21	20	13	38	2	45
Exodus	1972	22	15	18	45	28	13
Mound	1964	23	24	49	2	3	42
Communitas 2	1947	24	41	1	4	41	35
Satellite City	1965	25	23	32	29	13	29
Levittown	1958	26	28	22	19	37	22
Garden City	1902	27	26	28	24	34	19
Tokyo Bay	1960	28	27	3	43	30	28
Convention City	1972	29	31	33	5	43	21
Savannah	1733	30	22	30	33	32	17
Rush City Reformed	1923	31	25	31	27	26	27
Agricultural City	1960	32	30	39	7	38	24
Bridge-Town Over the Channel	1963	33	21	29	48	18	25
Brasilia	1957	34	43	20	12	33	37
Ratingen-West	1965	35	42	35	14	16	43
Phalanstère	1800	36	34	40	13	31	33
Handloser Project	1973	37	44	23	6	39	39
Marienburg	1890	38	33	38	26	23	34
Zarzis Resort	1974	39	35	46	21	19	40
Ocean City	1960	40	38	11	44	40	31
Cite Industrielle	1917	41	36	27	36	27	38
Chicago	1940	42	49	4	16	49	49
Clusters in the Air	1962	43	32	45	49	21	30
Roadtown	1910	44	45	47	3	46	41
Broadacre City	1934	45	48	37	10	44	47
Neuf-Brisach	1700	46	39	43	37	36	36
Jeffersonville	1802	47	40	42	32	48	32
Earthships	1970	48	46	44	15	45	44
Saltworks	1775	49	47	48	17	47	46

POPULATION DENSITY

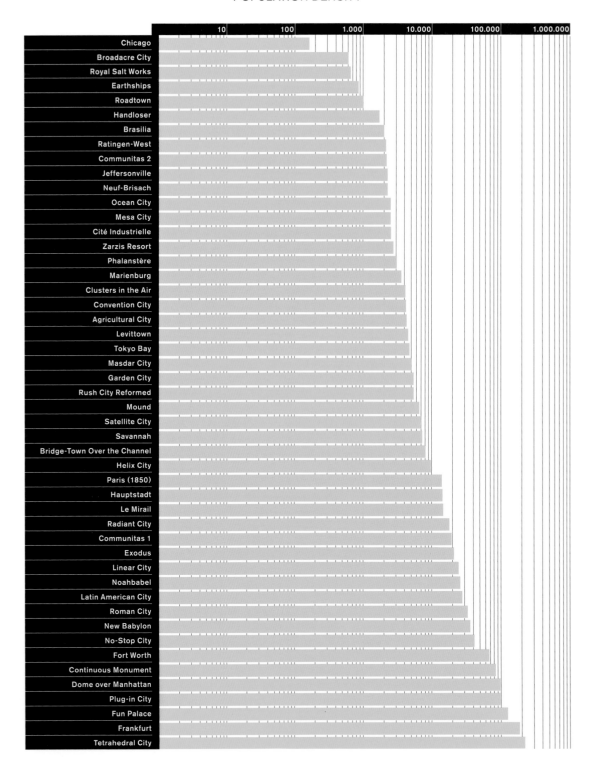

TOTAL POPULATION

	10	100	1.000	10.000	100.000	1.000.000	10.000.000
Mound							
Royal Salt Works							
Zarzis Resort							
Roadtown							
Clusters in the Air							
Earthships							
Fun Palace							
Neuf-Brisach							
Jeffersonville							
Phalanstère							
Agricultural City							
Marienburg							
Broadacre City							
Frankfurt							
Ratingen-West							
No-Stop City							
Convention City							
Satellite City							
Rush City Reformed							
Bridge-Town Over the Channel							
Savannah							
Masdar City							
Garden City							
Cité Industrielle							
Le Mirail							
Linear City							
Roman City							
Handloser							
Levittown							
Noahbabel							
Fort Worth							
Hauptstadt							
Brasilia							
Exodus							
Latin American City							
Plug-in City							
Helix City							
New Babylon							
Ocean City							
Dome over Manhattan							
Continuous Monument							
Tetrahedral City							
Paris (1850)							
Mesa City							
Radiant City							
Chicago							
Tokyo Bay							
Communitas 1							
Communitas 2							

% GREENSPACE

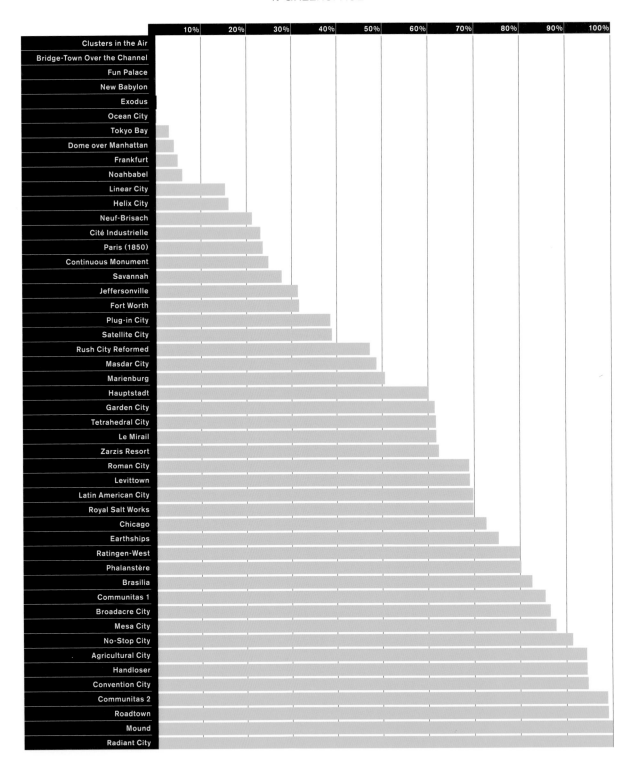

% PARKLAND

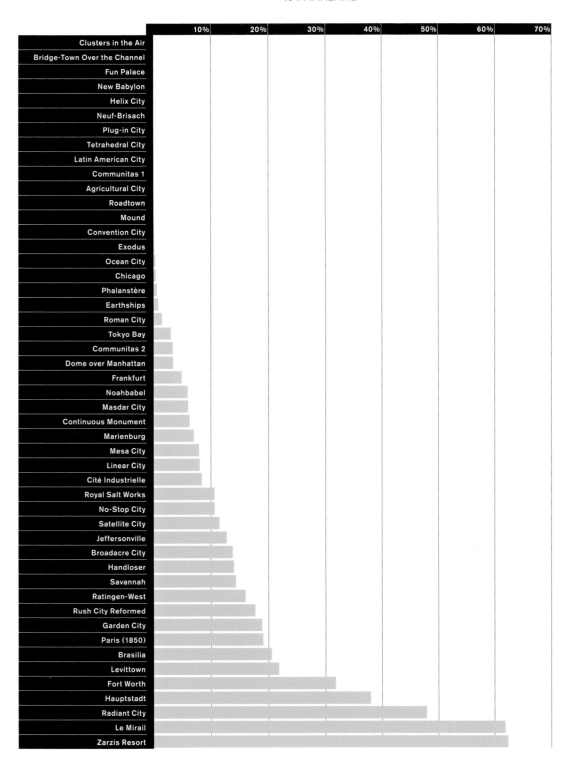

2D DENSITY: BY LAND USE

	10	100	1.000	10.000	100.000	1.000.000

Chicago
Broadacre City
Royal Salt Works
Earthships
Roadtown
Handloser
Brasilia
Ratingen-West
Communitas 2
Jeffersonville
Neuf-Brisach
Ocean City
Mesa City
Cité Industrielle
Zarzis Resort
Phalanstère
Marienburg
Clusters in the Air
Convention City
Agricultural City
Masdar City
Levittown
Tokyo Bay
Garden City
Rush City Reformed
Mound
Satellite City
Savannah
Bridge-Town Over the Channel
Helix City
Paris (1850)
Hauptstadt
Le Mirail
Radiant City
Communitas 1
Exodus
Linear City
Noahbabel
Latin American City
Roman City
New Babylon
No-Stop City
Fort Worth
Continuous Monument
Dome over Manhattan
Plug-in City
Fun Palace
Frankfurt
Tetrahedral City

DENSITY (2-D)   DENSITY (3-D)

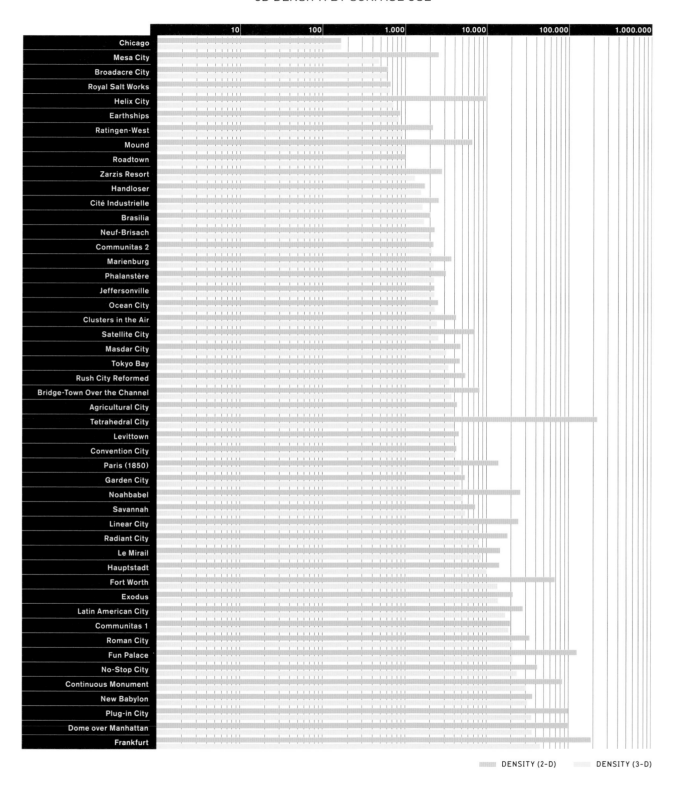

DENSITY (2-D)   DENSITY (3-D)

FLOOR AREA RATIO: 3D AREA/2D AREA

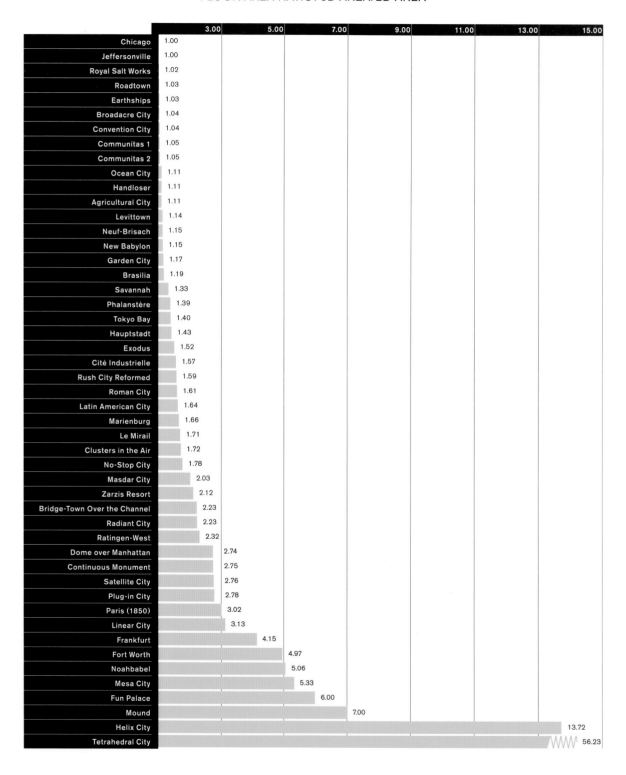

	3.00	5.00	7.00	9.00	11.00	13.00	15.00
Chicago	1.00						
Jeffersonville	1.00						
Royal Salt Works	1.02						
Roadtown	1.03						
Earthships	1.03						
Broadacre City	1.04						
Convention City	1.04						
Communitas 1	1.05						
Communitas 2	1.05						
Ocean City	1.11						
Handloser	1.11						
Agricultural City	1.11						
Levittown	1.14						
Neuf-Brisach	1.15						
New Babylon	1.15						
Garden City	1.17						
Brasilia	1.19						
Savannah	1.33						
Phalanstère	1.39						
Tokyo Bay	1.40						
Hauptstadt	1.43						
Exodus	1.52						
Cité Industrielle	1.57						
Rush City Reformed	1.59						
Roman City	1.61						
Latin American City	1.64						
Marienburg	1.66						
Le Mirail	1.71						
Clusters in the Air	1.72						
No-Stop City	1.78						
Masdar City	2.03						
Zarzis Resort	2.12						
Bridge-Town Over the Channel	2.23						
Radiant City	2.23						
Ratingen-West	2.32						
Dome over Manhattan		2.74					
Continuous Monument		2.75					
Satellite City		2.76					
Plug-in City		2.78					
Paris (1850)		3.02					
Linear City		3.13					
Frankfurt		4.15					
Fort Worth		4.97					
Noahbabel		5.06					
Mesa City		5.33					
Fun Palace		6.00					
Mound		7.00					
Helix City						13.72	
Tetrahedral City							56.23

SITE AREA (M²)

	10	100	1.000	10.000	100.000	1.000.000	10^6	10^7	10^8	10^9	10^{10}
Mound											
Fun Palace											
Frankfurt											
Zarzis Resort											
Clusters in the Air											
No-Stop City											
Royal Salt Works											
Neuf-Brisach											
Jeffersonville											
Roadtown											
Phalanstère											
Agricultural City											
Fort Worth											
Roman City											
Marienburg											
Linear City											
Earthships											
Le Mirail											
Satellite City											
Noahbabel											
Plug-in City											
Bridge-Town Over the Channel											
Rush City Reformed											
Savannah											
Tetrahedral City											
Convention City											
Garden City											
Masdar City											
Ratingen-West											
Hauptstadt											
Exodus											
Latin American City											
Dome over Manhattan											
Broadacre City											
Continuous Monument											
New Babylon											
Cité Industrielle											
Levittown											
Handloser											
Helix City											
Brasilia											
Paris (1850)											
Radiant City											
Ocean City											
Communitas 1											
Mesa City											
Tokyo Bay											
Communitas 2											
Chicago											

DENSITY VS. BUILT AREA

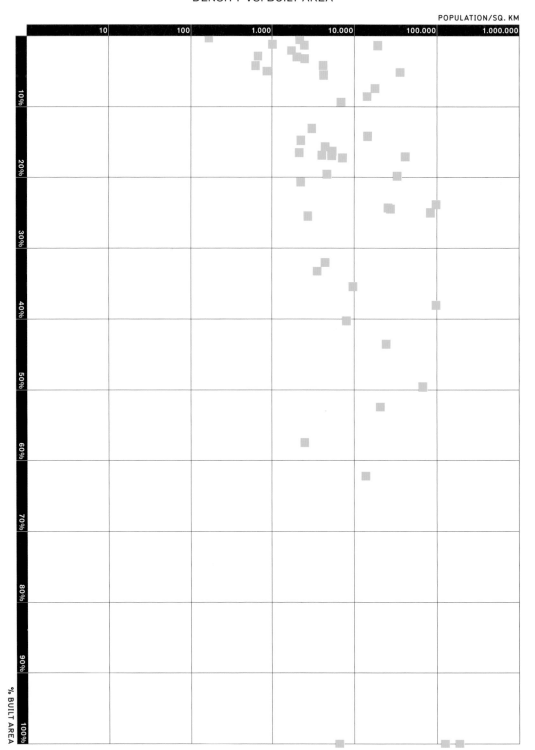

DENSITY VS. GREENSPACE

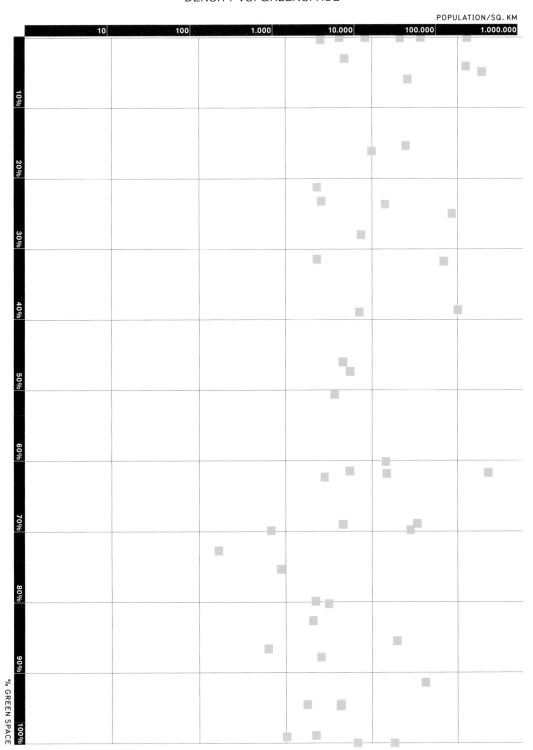

SOURCES

ROMAN CITY

Brown, Frank Edward. *Roman Architecture.* New York: G. Braziller, 1961.

Clarke, John R. *The Houses of Roman Italy, 100BC–AD250: Ritual, Space and Decoration.* Berkeley, Calif.: University of California Press, 1991.

Goodman, Penelope J. *The Roman City and its Periphery: From Rome to Gaul.* London, New York: Routledge, 2007.

Hales, Shelley. *The Roman House and Social Identity.* New York: Cambridge University Press, 2003.

Liebeschuetz, J.H.W.G. *The Decline and Fall of the Roman City.* Oxford, New York: Oxford University Press, 2000.

Lorenz, Thuri. *Roemische Staedte.* Darmstadt: Wissenschaftliche Buchgesellschaft, 1987.

Macaulay, David. *City: A Story of Roman Planning and Construction.* Boston: Houghton Mifflin Company, 1974.

McKay, Alexander Gordon. *Houses, Villas and Palaces in the Roman World.* Baltimore: Johns Hopkins University Press, 1998.

Merrifield, Ralph. *The Roman City of London.* London: E. Benn, 1965.

Nash, Ernest. *Roman Towns.* New York, J. J. Augustin, 1944.

Owens, J.E. *The City in the Greek and Roman World.* London, New York: Routledge, 1991.

Stambaugh, John E. *The Ancient Roman City.* Baltimore: Johns Hopkins University Press, 1988.

LATIN AMERICAN CITY

Markman, Sidney David. *Architecture and Urbanization of Colonial Central America.* Tempe: Ariz.: Center for Latin American Studies, Arizona State University, 1993

Martinez Lemoine, Rene. "The Classical Model of the Spanish-American Colonial City." *The Journal of Architecture* Santiago, Chile: 2002.

Rotenberg, Robert; McDonough, Gary. *The Cultural Meaning of Urban Space.* London: Bergin and Garvey, 1993.

Smith, Robert. "Colonial Towns of Spanish and Portuguese America." *The Journal of the Society of Architectural Historians* vol. 14 no. 4, Town Planning Issue (Dec. 1955), pp. 3–12.

NEUF-BRISACH

Bornecque, Robert. *La France de Vauban.* Paris: Arthaud, 1984.

SAVANNAH

Bacon, Edmund N. *The Design of Cities.* New York: Viking Press, 1974.

Bannister, Turpin C. "Oglethorpe's Sources for the Savannah Plan." *Journal of the Society of Architectural Historians* vol. 20 (May 1961), pp. 47–62.

ROYAL SALT WORKS

Vidler, Anthony. *Claude-Nicolas Ledoux: Architecture and Social Reform at the End of the Ancien Régime.* Cambridge, Mass.: MIT Press, 1990.

Vidler, Anthony. *Claude-Nicolas Ledoux: Architecture and Utopia in the Era of the French Revolution.* Basel, Boston: Birkhäuser-Publishers for Architecture, 2006.

PHALANSTÈRE

Forrest, Aaron. "The North American Phalanx: Ideology and Institution." Paper for Princeton University ARC 548–Histories and Theories of Architecture: 18th and 19th Centuries. January 2006.

Fourier, Charles. *Design for Utopia: Selected Writings of Charles Fourier.* New York: Schocken Books, 1971.

Riasanovsky, Nicholas V. *The Teaching of Charles Fourier.* Berkeley: University of California Press, 1969.

JEFFERSONVILLE

Reps, John W. "Thomas Jefferson's Checkerboard Towns." *The Journal of the Society of Architectural Historians,* vol. 20, no. 3 (Oct. 1961), pp. 108–114.

PARIS (1850)

Gandy, Matthew. "The Paris Sewers and the Rationalization of Urban Space." *Transactions of the Institute of British Geographers,* New Series, vol. 24, no. 1. (1999), pp. 23–44.

Pinkney, David H. "Napoleon III's Transformation of Paris: The Origins and Development of the Idea." *The Journal of Modern History,* vol. 27, no. 2. (Jun. 1955), pp. 125–134.

Saalman, Howard. *Haussmann: Paris Transformed.* New York: G. Braziller, 1971.

Haussmann. *Mémoires du Baron Haussmann.* Paris: Victor-Havard, 1890–93.

MARIENBURG

Sitte, Camillo. *The Art of Building Cities: City Building According to its Artistic Fundamentals.* Westport, Conn.: Hyperion Press, 1979.

Sommer, Richard M. "Beyond Centers, 'Fabric,' and the Culture of Congestion: Urban Design as a Metropolitan Enterprise." *Harvard Design Magazine* no. 25 (Fall 2006–Winter 2007), pp. 50–59.

GARDEN CITY

Howard, Ebenezer. *Garden Cities of To-morrow.* London: Faber and Faber Ltd., 1945.

ROAD TOWN

Sky, Alison and Michelle Stone. *Unbuilt America.* New York: McGraw-Hill, 1976.

Chambless, Edgar. *Roadtown.* New York: Roadtown Press, 1910.

CITÉ INDUSTRIELLE

Wiebenson, Dora. *Tony Garnier: The Cité Industrielle.* New York: G. Braziller, 1970.

RUSH CITY REFORMED

Sky, Alison and Michelle Stone. *Unbuilt America.* New York: McGraw-Hill, 1976.

BROADACRE CITY

Wright, Frank Lloyd. *The Living City.* New York: Horizon Press, 1958.

RADIANT CITY

Le Corbusier. *The City of Tomorrow and its Planning.* London: J. Rodker 1929.

Le Corbusier. *Towards a New Architecture.* London: Architectural Press, 1948.

Le Corbusier. *Radiant City.* London: Faber, 1967.

McLeod, Mary. "La Ferme Radieuse, Le Village Radieux," *Le Corbusier et La Nature.* Paris: Fondation Le Corbusier, 1996.

Samuel, Godfrey. "Radiant City and Garden Suburb." *Journal of RIBA,* v. 43 (Apr. 4, 1936), pp. 595–599.

CHICAGO

Hilberseimer, Ludwig. *The Nature of Cities; Origin, Growth, and Decline, Pattern and Form, Planning Problems.* Chicago: P. Theobald, 1955.

Hilberseimer, Ludwig. *The New City; Principles of Planning.* Chicago: P. Theobald, 1944.

Hilberseimer, Ludwig. *The New Regional Pattern; Industries and Gardens, Workshops and Farms.* Chicago: P. Theobald, 1949.

COMMUNITAS 1

Goodman, Paul and Percival Goodman. *Communitas.* Chicago: University of Chicago Press: 1947. pp. 59–123.

COMMUNITAS 2

Goodman, Paul and Percival Goodman. *Communitas.* Chicago: University of Chicago Press: 1947. pp. 59–123.

LEVITTOWN

Gans, Herbert. J. *The Levittowners: Ways of Life and Politics in a New Suburban Community.* New York: Pantheon Books, 1967.

Keller, Mollie. *Levittown and the Transformation of the Metropolis.* Doctoral dissertation, New York University, 1990.

FORT WORTH

Gruen, Victor. *The Heart of Our Cities.* The Urban Crisis: Diagnosis and Cure. New York: Simon and Schuster, 1964.

Gruen, Victor. *Centers for the Urban Environment. Survival of the Cities.* New York: Van Nostrand Reinhold Co., 1973.

Gruen, Victor. *East Island: A Proposal for the Conversion of Welfare Island, New York, to a Residential Community.* New York, 1961.

BRASILIA

Willy Stäeubli. *Brasilia.* New York: Universe Books, 1966.

HAUPTSTADT

Smithson, Alison & Peter, *The Charged Void: Urbanism.* New York: Monacelli Press, 2005.

Smithson, Alison & Peter, *The Charged Void: Architecture.* New York: Monacelli Press, 2005.

Risselada, Max & Dirk Van Den Heuvel, *Team 10: 1953–81, In Search of a Utopia of the Present.* Rotterdam: NAi Publishers, 2005.

AGRICULTURAL CITY

"Helix Plan" and "Agricultural City." *Space Design,* no. 163 (April 1978), pp. 110–113.

Kurokawa, Kisho. *Philosophy of Urban Design and Its Planning Method* Tokyo: Shokokusha, 1995.

Kurokawa, Kisho. *Retrospective Kurokawa Kisho.* Paris: Maison de la Culture du Japon a Paris, 1998.

Kurokawa, Kisho. *Kisho Kurokawa: From the Age of the Machine to the Age of Life.* Ed Dennis Sharp. London: BookART, 1998.

BRIDGE-TOWN OVER THE CHANNEL

Schulze-Fielitz, Eckhard. "Un Theorie pour l'occupation de l'espace." *L'Architecture d'ajourd'hui* (July 1962).

Lebesque, Sabine and Helene Fentener van Vlissingen. *Yona Friedman: Structures Serving the Unpredictable.* Rotterdam: NAi Publishers, 1999.

DOME OVER MANHATTAN

Martin, Reinhold: "Forget Fuller?" ANY: Everything You Always Wanted to Know About Fuller but Were Afraid to Ask. #17, 1997.

Fuller, Buckminster R. "A Collection of Articles and Papers on Design." *50 Years of the Design Science Revolution and the World Game.* Carbondale, IL: World Resources Inventory, 1969.

Fuller, Buckminster R. and Robert Marks. *The Dymaxion World of Buckminster Fuller.* Carbondale: Southern Illinois University Press, 1960.

MESA CITY

Soleri, Paolo. *Architecture as Human Ecology.* New York, NY: The Monacelli Press, 2003.

Soleri, Paolo. *Arcology: The City in the Image of Man.* Cambridge, Mass.: MIT Press, 1969.

"Quella Che Soleri Chiama Arcologia: Architettura + Ecologia." *Domus* (1969).

NEW BABYLON

Wigley, Mark. *Constant's New Babylon: The Hyper-architecture of Desire.* Rotterdam: Witte de With, Center for Contemporary Art: 010 Publishers, 1998.

OCEAN CITY

"Tokyo 1964." *Architectural Design,* v. 34 (Oct. 1964).

"Ocean City." *World Architecture,* n. 2 (1965), pp. 26–27.

Ross, Michael Franklin. *Beyond Metabolism: The New Japanese Architecture.* New York: Architectural Record Books, 1978.

TOKYO BAY

Tange, Kenzo. *Kenzo Tange, 1946–1996: Architecture and Urban Design.* Ed. Massimo Bettinotti. Milan: Electa 1996.

"Tokyo 1964." *Architectural Design,* v. 34 (Oct. 1964).

Ross, Michael Franklin. *Beyond Metabolism: The New Japanese Architecture.* New York: Architectural Record Books, 1978.

HELIX CITY

"Helix Plan" and "Agricultural City." *Space Design* no. 163 (April 1978), pp. 110–113.

Kurokawa, Kisho. *Philosophy of Urban Design and Its Planning Method* Tokyo: Shokokusha, 1995.

Kurokawa, Kisho. *Retrospective Kurokawa Kisho.* Paris: Maison de la Culture du Japon a Paris, 1998.

Kurokawa, Kisho. *Kisho Kurokawa: From the Age of the Machine to the Age of Life.* Ed Dennis Sharp. London: BookART, 1998.

CLUSTERS IN THE AIR

Stewart, David B. *Arata Isozaki: Architecture, 1960–1990.* New York: Rizzoli, 1991.

Isozaki, Arata. *Arata Isozaki Works 30 Architectural Models, Prints, Drawings.* Tokyo: Rikuyo-sha Publishing, Inc, 1992. pp. 19–29.

Isozaki, Arata. *Unbuilt.* Tokyo: TOTO Shuppan, 2001. pp. 32–81.

LE MIRAIL

Candilis, Georges. *Toulouse le Mirail: Birth of a New Town.* Dokumente der modernen Architektur; Stuttgart: K. Kramer, 1975.

Smithson, Peter. "Toulouse le Mirail" *Architectural Design,* v. 41 (Oct. 1971), pp. 599–604.

FRANKFURT

Avermaete, Tom. *Another Modern, The Post-War Architecture and Urbanism of Candilis-Josic-Woods.* Rotterdam: NAi Publishers, 2005.

Risselada, Max & Dirk Van Den Heuvel. *Team 10: 1953–81, in Search of a Utopia of the Present.* Rotterdam: NAi Publishers, 2005.

MOUND

Spens, Michael. "From Mound to Sponge: How Peter Cook Explores Landscape Buildings." *Architectural Design,* vol. 77 (March 2007), pp. 12–15.

PLUG-IN CITY

Cook, Peter. *Archigram.* New York: Princeton Architectural Press, 1999.

Sadler, Simon. *Archigram: Architecture Without Architecture.* Cambridge, Mass.: MIT Press, 2005.

FUN PALACE

Price, Cedric. *Cedric Price: The Square Book.* London: Academy Editions; Chichester: John Wiley, 2003.

Price, Cedric. *Cedric Price.* London: Architectural Association, 1984.

RATINGEN-WEST

Moholy-Nagy, Sybil. *Matrix of Man: An Illustrated History of Urban Environment.* New York: Praeger, 1968.

Mattern, Merete. "Centre de Ratingen-West, 1965". *Aujourd'hui, art et architecture,* vol. 10 (Oct. 1967), pp. 134, 139.

SATELLITE CITY

Koenig, Giovanni. "L'esecutivo dell'utopia (Carrying out Utopia): Manfredi Nicoletti." *Casabella,* no. 347 (1970), p. 17.

TETRAHEDRAL CITY

Fuller, Buckminster R. "A Collection of Articles and Papers on Design." *50 Years of the Design Science Revolution and the World Game.* Carbondale, IL: World Resources Inventory, 1969.

Fuller, Buckminster R. and Robert Marks. *The Dymaxion World of Buckminster Fuller.* Carbondale: Southern Illinois University Press, 1960.

LINEAR CITY

Huxtable, Ada Louise. "How to Build a City, if You Can," *Forum,* vol. 20 (March 1968).

Moholy-Nagy, Sybil. *Matrix of a Man: An Illustrated History of Urban Environment.* New York: F.A. Praeger, 1968.

CONTINUOUS MONUMENT

van Schaik, Martin and Mácel, Otaker. *Exit Utopia: Architectural Provocations, 1956–1976.* Munich; London: Prestel, 2004.

Lang, Peter and Menking, William. *Superstudio: Life Without Objects.* Milan: Skira, 2003.

Superstudio. "Premonizioni della Parusia Urbanistica: 12 Ideal Cities." *Casabella* (Mar. 1972).

NO-STOP CITY

Archizoom Associates. "No-stop City, Residential Parkings, Climatic Universal System." *Domus,* no. 496 (March 1971), pp. 49–54.

Branzi, Andrea. *No-Stop City.* Orléans: HYX, 2006.

Branzi, Andrea. "Il ruolo dell'avanguardia" *Casabella,* vol. 36 (March 1972), pp. 27–33; (April 1972), pp. 31–38.

Hays, Michael. *Architecture Theory Since 1968.* Cambridge, Mass: The MIT Press, 1998.

Jencks, Charles. "The Supersensualists II." *Architectural Design* (January 1972), pp. 18–21.

Staufer, Marie Theres. "Utopian Reflections, Reflected Utopias: Urban Designs by Archizoom and Superstudio." *AA Files* (Summer 2002), pp. 23–36.

van Schaik, Martin and Mácel, Otaker. *Exit Utopia: Architectural Provocations, 1956–1976.* Munich, London: Prestel, 2004.

NOAHBABEL

Soleri, Paolo. *Architecture as Human Ecology.* New York, NY: The Monacelli Press, 2003.

Soleri, Paolo. *Arcology: The City in the Image of Man.* Cambridge, Mass.: MIT Press, 1969.

"Quella Che Soleri Chiama Arcologia: Architettura + Ecologia." *Domus* (1969).

EARTHSHIPS

Reynolds, Michael E. *Earthship.* Taos, N.M.: Solar Survival Architecture, 1990.

CONVENTION CITY

Ant Farm. *Truck Stop.* Sausalito: Ant Farm Inc., 1971.

Lewallen, Constance. *Ant Farm, 1968–1978.* Berkeley: University of California Press, Berkeley Art Museum, Pacific Film Archive, 2004.

EXODUS

Van Schaik, Martin and Mácel, Otaker. *Exit Utopia: Architectural Provocations, 1956–1976.* Munich; London: Prestel, 2004.

HANDLOSER

Snibbe, Richard W. *The Handloser Project: A New Town of 60,000 People to be Built in a Mountainous Area.* New York: Snibbe, 1973.

ZARZIS RESORT

Costantino Dardi: testimonianze e riflessioni. Ed. Michele Costanzo. Milano: Electa, 1992.

"Italie '75" *L'Architecture D'Aujourd'hui* (Sep/Oct. 1975), pp. 54–55.

MASDAR CITY

www.masdaruae.com

www.fosterandpartners.com/News/291/Default.aspx

www.worldarchitecturenews.com/index.php?fuseaction=wannappln.projectview&upload_id=10064

49 CITIES
is published by
Inventory Press, LLC
167 Bowery, 3rd floor
New York, NY 10002
inventorypress.com

EDITOR
Eugenia Bell

DESIGN
Project Projects

Third Edition
© 2015 WORK Architecture Company

IMAGE CREDITS
pp. 13, 46: The Frank Lloyd Wright Foundation
Archives (The Museum of Modern Art | Avery
Architectural & Fine Arts Library, Columbia
University, New York); p. 14: Photo by Raymond
Adams; p. 15: courtesy WORKac; p. 48:
© F.L.C. / ADAGP, Paris / Artists Rights Society
(ARS), New York 2015; pp. 55, 126–128:
Images Courtesy of Chip Lord; pp. 66, 129–130:
© Yona Friedman; p. 68: Image Courtesy the
Estate of R. Buckminster Fuller; p. 80: Yoshio
Takase / GA Photographers; p. 90: Cedric
Price fonds, Canadian Centre for Architecture,
Montréal; p. 100: © CNAC/MNAM/Dist. RMN-
Grand Palais / Art Resource, NY © Gian Piero
Frassinelli; p. 116: Foster + Partners, Nigel
Young / Foster + Partners; p. 125: courtesy of
Berkeley Art Museum and Paciifc Film Archives

Distributed in North America by
RAM Publications
2525 Michigan Avenue,
Bldg. #A2
Santa Monica, CA 90404
rampub.com

Distributed in Europe by
Anagram Books
anagrambooks.com
contact@anagrambooks.com

ISBN: 978-1-941753-05-7

PRINTING
Printed by Szaransky, Poland

PROJECT TEAM
Amale Andraos
Dan Wood
Yasmin Vobis
Michael Alexander
Hilary Zaic
Jose Esparza
Anne Menke
Sam Dufaux
Jenny Lie Andersen
Alexander Maymind
Willem Boning

This project was made possible through an
Independent Project grant from the New York
State Council on the Arts and the generosity of
the Brightman Hill Charitable Foundation.

First and second editions of
49 CITIES
were published by
Storefront for Art and Architecture
www.storefrontnews.org

SPECIAL THANKS TO
Peter Guggenheimer
Lauren Kogod
Princeton University School of Architecture
Stan Allen
Joseph Grima
Susannah Bohlke
Project Projects
Adam Michaels
Nikki Chung
Molly Sherman
Shannon Harvey
Grace Robinson-Leo
Siiri Tännler

and all of our Kickstarter backers
for their incredible support.